Fundamentals of Project Management

Fourth Edition

Fundamentals of Project Management

Fourth Edition

JOSEPH HEAGNEY

American Management Association
New York • Atlanta • Brussels • Chicago • Mexico City • San Francisco
Shanghai • Tokyo • Toronto • Washington, D.C.

This publication is designed to provide accurate and authoritative information in regard to the subject matter covered. It is sold with the understanding that the publisher is not engaged in rendering legal, accounting, or other professional service. If legal advice or other expert assistance is required, the services of a competent professional person should be sought.

"PMI" and the PMI logo are service and trademarks of the Project Management Institute, Inc. which are registered in the United States of America and other nations; "PMP" and the PMP logo are certification marks of the Project Management Institute, Inc. which are registered in the United States of America and other nations; "PMBOK", "PM Network", and "PMI Today" are trademarks of the Project Management Institute, Inc. which are registered in the United States of America and other nations; ". . . building professionalism in project management . . ." is a trade and service mark of the Project Management Institute, Inc. which is registered in the United States of America and other nations; and the Project Management Journal logo is a trademark of the Project Management Institute, Inc.

PMI did not participate in the development of this publication and has not reviewed the content for accuracy. PMI does not endorse or otherwise sponsor this publication and makes no warranty, guarantee, or representation, expressed or implied, as to its accuracy or content. PMI does not have any financial interest in this publication, and has not contributed any financial resources.

Additionally, PMI makes no warranty, guarantee, or representation, express or implied, that the successful completion of any activity or program, or the use of any product or publication, designed to prepare candidates for the PMP® Certification Examination, will result in the completion or satisfaction of any PMP® Certification eligibility requirement or standard.

Library of Congress Cataloging-in-Publication Data

Heagney, Joseph.
   Fundamentals of project management / Joseph Heagney.—4th ed.
     p. cm.
     Includes bibliographical references and index.
     ISBN-13: 978-0-8144-1748-5
     ISBN-10: 0-8144-1748-5
     1. Project management.   I. Title.
   HD69.P75L488   2011
   658.4'04—dc22

                                     2011012421

Printing number
10 9 8 7 6 5 4 3 2

To the memory of Mackenzie Joseph Heagney,
sleeping with the angels.

CONTENTS

FIGURE LIST

Preface to the Fourth Edition

Sending a satellite to Mars? Planning a conference or implementing new software? You have chosen the right book. The great value of project management is that it can be applied across industries and situations alike, on multiple levels. It would be difficult to find a more nimble organizational discipline. Whether or not your title says project manager, you can benefit from the practical applications presented in this book, which is intended as a brief overview of the tools, techniques, and discipline of project management as a whole. Three notable topics have been expanded for this edition, with new chapters on the project manager as leader, managing project risk, and the change control process. Although each topic is important individually, together they can establish the basis for project success or failure.

Projects are often accomplished by teams, teams are made up of people, and people are driven by . . . project leaders. Conspicuously absent from the preceding is the term "manager," as in "project manager." If project managers manage projects, what do they do with the people who make up their teams or support networks in the absence of a formal team? Successful project leaders *lead* the people on their teams to consistent goal attainment and enhanced performance. They combine a command of project tools and technical savvy with a real understanding of leadership and team performance. Consistently successful projects depend on both. It is a balancing act of execution and skilled people management. Ignoring one or the other is inviting project failure and organizational inconsistency regarding project performance.

Risk is an element inherent in every project. The project manager must consider several variables when determining how much to invest in the mitigation and management of that risk. How experienced is my team or support personnel? Do I have the appropriate skill sets available? Can I count on reliable data from previous projects, or am I wandering in the wilderness? Whatever the assessment, project risk is something that needs to be addressed early in the life of the project. As with any other process you will be introduced to in this book, risk must be managed formally, with little deviation from the template, while allowing for some flexibility. Project managers cannot afford to wait for bad things to happen and then fix them. Reactive management is too costly. The practical Six-Step process presented on pages 57–62 can and should be applied to any project. How it is applied directly depends on the variables that confront that project.

Death, taxes, and change. Project managers need to expand the list of certainties in life. To paraphrase James P. Lewis, author of the first three editions of this book, in Chapter 3, project failures are caused primarily by the failure to plan properly. I often tell my seminar attendees that planning is everything and that most projects succeed or fail up front. This is not an overstatement. But what often gets lost in project execution is the absolute necessity to keep the plan current based on the changes that have affected the project from day one. Have the changes affected the scope of the project? Has the schedule or budget been impacted in any significant way? These are the questions that must be asked and answered when applying effective change control to the project. Failure to manage and communicate change results in serious misalignment and probably failure. Chapter 10 presents the reader with a practical change control process that can help ensure project success.

As a former Global Practice Leader for project management at the American Management Association, I had the luxury of benchmarking multiple organizations worldwide and identified several project-related best practices. The applications discussed here represent some of those practices, as well as those presented in the latest version of the *PMBOK® Guide*. With this expanded edition of *Fundamentals of Project Management*, I hope to enhance your chances of bringing projects in on time, on budget with an excellent deliverable—every time.

Joseph J. Heagney
Sayville, NY
February 2011

Acknowledgments

A special thanks to Nicolle Heagney for her technical assistance in creating many of the figures and charts presented in the book. Her expertise and diligence made my life a lot easier.

Thanks to Kyle Heagney for allowing me to miss some of his soccer games.

Fundamentals of Project Management

Fourth Edition

CHAPTER 1

An Overview of Project Management

W hat's all the fuss about, anyway? Since the first edition of this book was published, in 1997, the Project Management Institute (PMI®) has grown from a few thousand members to nearly 450,000 in 2011. For those of you who don't know, PMI is the professional organization for people who manage projects. You can get more information from the institute's website, *www.pmi.org*. In addition to providing a variety of member services, a major objective of PMI is to advance project management as a profession. To do so, it has established a certification process whereby qualifying individuals receive the Project Management Professional (PMP®) designation. To do so, such individuals must have work experience (approximately five thousand hours) and pass an online exam that is based on the *Project Management Body of Knowledge*, or the *PMBOK® Guide*.

A professional association? Just for project management? Isn't project management just a variant on general management?

Yes and no. There are a lot of similarities, but there are enough differences to justify treating project management as a discipline separate from general management. For one thing, projects are more schedule-intensive than most of the activities that general managers handle. And the people in a project team often don't report directly to the project manager, whereas they do report to most general managers.

So just what is project management, and, for that matter, what is a project? PMI defines a project as "a temporary endeavor undertaken to produce a unique product, service, or result" (*PMBOK® Guide*, Project Management Institute, 2008, p. 5). This means that a project is done only one time. If it is repetitive, it's not a project. A project should have definite starting and ending points (time), a budget (cost), a clearly defined scope—or magnitude—of work to be done, and specific performance requirements that must be met. I say "should" because seldom does a project conform to the desired definition. These constraints on a project, by the way, are referred to throughout this book as the PCTS targets.

> **PMI defines a project as ". . . a temporary endeavor undertaken to produce a unique product, service, or result."**

Dr. J. M. Juran, the quality guru, also defines a *project* as a problem scheduled for solution. I like this definition because it reminds me that every project is conducted to solve some kind of problem for a company. However, I must caution that the word "problem" typically has a negative meaning, and projects deal with both positive and negative kinds of problems. For example, developing a new product is a problem, but a positive one, while an environmental cleanup project deals with a negative kind of problem.

> **A project is a problem scheduled for solution.**
>
> —J. M. Juran

Project Failures

In fact, the Standish Group (*www.standishgroup.com*) has found that only about 17 percent of all software projects done in the

United States meet the original PCTS targets, 50 percent must have the targets changed—meaning they are usually late or overspent and must have their performance requirements reduced—and the remaining 33 percent are actually canceled. One year, U.S. companies spent more than $250 billion on software development nationwide, so this means that $80 billion was completely lost on canceled projects. What is truly astonishing is that 83 percent of all software projects get into trouble!

Now, lest you think I am picking on software companies, let me say that these statistics apply to many different kinds of projects. Product development, for example, shares similar dismal rates of failure, waste, and cancellation. Experts on product development estimate that about 30 percent of the cost to develop a new product is rework. That means that one of every three engineers assigned to a project is working full time just redoing what two other engineers did wrong in the first place!

I also have a colleague, Bob Dudley, who has been involved in construction projects for thirty-five years. He tells me that these jobs also tend to have about 30 percent rework, a fact that I found difficult to believe, because I have always thought of construction as being fairly well defined and thus easier to control than might be the case for research projects, for example. Nevertheless, several colleagues of mine confirm Bob's statistics.

The reason for these failures is consistently found to be inadequate project planning. People adopt a ready-fire-aim approach in an effort to get a job done really fast and end up spending far more time than necessary by reworking errors, recovering from diversions down "blind alleys," and so on.

I am frequently asked how to justify formal project management to senior managers in companies, and I always cite these statistics. However, they want to know whether using good project management really reduces the failures and the rework, and I can only say you will have to try it and see for yourself. If you can achieve levels of rework of only a few percent using a seat-of-the-pants approach to managing projects, then keep doing what you're doing! However, I don't believe you will find this to be true.

The question I would ask is whether general management makes a difference. If we locked up all the managers in a company for a couple of months, would business continue at the same levels of performance, or would those levels decline? If they decline, then we could argue that management must have been doing something positive, and vice versa. I doubt that many general managers would want to say that what they do doesn't matter. However, we all know that there are effective and ineffective general managers, and this is true of project managers, as well.

What Is Project Management?

The *PMBOK® Guide* definition of *project management* is "application of knowledge, skills, tools, and techniques to project activities to meet the project requirements. Project management is accomplished through the application and integration of the 42 logically grouped project management processes comprising the 5 Process Groups: initiating, planning, executing, monitoring and controlling, and closing" (*PMBOK® Guide*, Project Management Institute, 2008, p. 6). Project requirements include the PCTS targets mentioned previously. The various processes of initiating, planning, and so on are addressed later in this chapter, and the bulk of this book is devoted to explaining how these processes are accomplished.

> **Project management is application of knowledge, skills, tools, and techniques to project activities to achieve project requirements. Project management is accomplished through the application and integration of the project management processes of initiating, planning, executing, monitoring and controlling, and closing.**

It would be better if the *PMBOK® Guide* specified that a project manager should *facilitate* planning. One mistake made by inexperienced project managers is to plan the project for the team. Not only do they get no buy-in to their plan, but that plan is usually full of holes. Managers can't think of everything, their estimates of task durations are wrong, and the entire thing falls apart after the project is started. The first rule of project management is that the people who must do the work should help plan it.

> **The first rule of project management is that the people who must do the work should help plan it.**

The role of the project manager is that of an enabler. Her job is to help the team get the work completed, to "run interference" for the team, to get scarce resources that team members need, and to buffer them from outside forces that would disrupt the work. She is not a project czar. She should be—above everything—a *leader*, in the true sense of the word.

The best definition of leadership that I have found is the one by Vance Packard, in his book *The Pyramid Climbers*. He says, "Leadership is the art of getting others to *want* to do something that you believe should be done." The operative word here is "want." Dictators get others to do things that they want done. So do guards who supervise prison work teams. But a leader gets people to want to do the work, and that is a significant difference.

> **"Leadership is the art of getting others to want to do something that you believe should be done."**
>
> —Vance Packard

The planning, scheduling, and control of work represent the management or administrative part of the job. But, without leadership, projects tend to just satisfy bare minimum requirements. With leadership, they can exceed those bare minimums. I offer a comprehensive application of project leadership techniques in Chapter 13.

It Is Not Just Scheduling!

One of the common misconceptions about project management is that it is just scheduling. At last report, Microsoft had sold a huge number of copies of Microsoft Project®, yet the project failure rate remains high. Scheduling is certainly a major tool used to manage projects, but it is not nearly as important as developing a shared understanding of what the project is supposed to accomplish or constructing a good work breakdown structure (WBS) to identify all the work to be done (I discuss the WBS in Chapter 6). In fact, without practicing good project management, the only thing a detailed schedule is going to do is allow you to document your failures with great precision!

I do want to make one point about scheduling software. It doesn't matter too much which package you select, as they all have strong and weak points. However, the tendency is to give people the software and expect them to learn how to use it without any training. This simply does not work. The features of scheduling software are such that most people don't learn the subtleties by themselves. They don't have the time, because they are trying to do their regular jobs, and not everyone is good at self-paced learning. You wouldn't hire a green person to run a complex machine in a factory and put him to work without training, because you know he will destroy something or injure himself. So why do it with software?

One-Person Projects

When is managing a project not project management? When only one person is involved.

A lot of people are sent to my seminars to learn how to manage projects, but they are the only person working on their projects. Now it is true that a one-person job can be called a project, because it has a definite starting point, target, end date, specific performance requirements, defined scope of work, and a budget. However, when no one else is working on the project (including outside vendors), there is no need for a critical path schedule. A critical path schedule is one that has a number of parallel paths, and one of them is longer than the others and determines how long it will take to complete the job or, ultimately, whether the given end date can be met. When you're working on a job by yourself, there aren't any parallel paths—unless you are ambidextrous!

One-person projects do require good self-management, or good time management, but all you need is a good to-do list, which comes from a task listing. However, unless you are coordinating the work of other people, you aren't practicing true project management.

The Big Trap—Working Project Managers

It is common to have individuals serve as project managers and require also that they do part of the actual work in the project. This is a certain prescription for problems. If it is a true team, consisting of several people, the project manager inevitably finds herself torn between managing and getting her part of the work done. Naturally, the work must take precedence, or the schedule will slip, so she opts to do the work. That means that the managing does not get done. She hopes it will take care of itself, but it never does. After all, if the team could manage itself, there would be no need for a project manager in the first place (remember our argument about whether project management matters?).

Unfortunately, when the time comes for her performance evaluation, she will be told that her managing needs improving. Actually, she just needs to be allowed to practice management in the first place.

Yes, for very small teams—perhaps up to three or four people—a project manager can do some of the work. But, as team sizes increase, it becomes impossible to work and manage both, because you are constantly being pulled away from the work by the needs of your team members.

One of the reasons for this situation is that organizations don't fully understand what project management is all about, and they think that it is possible for individuals to do both. The result is that nearly everyone in the company is trying to manage projects, and, as is true in every discipline, some of them will be good at it and others will have no aptitude whatsoever. I have found that a far better approach is to select a few individuals who have the aptitude and desire to be project managers and let them manage a number of small projects. This frees "technical" people (to use the term broadly) to do technical work without having to worry about administrative issues and allows project managers to get really good at their jobs.

It is outside the scope of this book to discuss how to select project managers, but, for the interested reader, the topic is covered in a book by Wysocki and Lewis titled *The World-Class Project Manager* (Perseus, 2001).

You Can't Have It All!

One of the common causes of project failures is that the project sponsor demands that the project manager must finish the job by a certain time, within budget, and at a given magnitude or scope, while achieving specific performance levels. In other words, the sponsor dictates all four of the project constraints. This doesn't work.

The relationship among the PCTS constraints can be written as follows:

$$C = f(P, T, S)$$

In words, this says, "Cost is a function of Performance, Time, and Scope." Graphically, I like to show it as a triangle, in which P, C, and T are the sides and S is the area. This is shown in Figure 1-1.

In geometry, we know that if we are given values for the sides of a triangle, we can compute the area. Or, if we know the area and the length of two sides, we can compute the length of the remaining side. This translates into a very practical rule of project management: The sponsor can assign values to any three variables, but the project manager must determine the remaining one.

Figure 1-1. Triangles showing the relationship between P, C, T, and S.

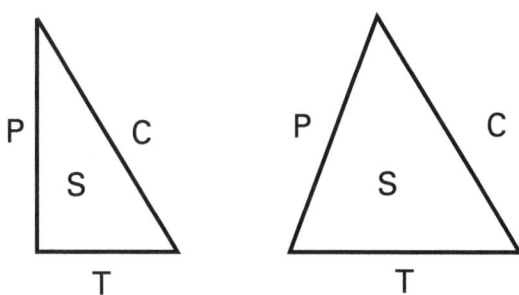

So let's assume that the sponsor requires certain performance, time, and scope from the project. It is the project manager's job to determine what it will cost to achieve those results. However, I always caution project managers that they should have a paramedic standing by when they give the cost figure to the sponsor because she will probably have a stroke or heart attack, and the paramedic will have to revive her.

Invariably, the sponsor exclaims, "How can it cost that much?" She had a figure in mind, and your number will always exceed her figure. And she may say, "If it's going to cost that much, we can't justify doing the job." Exactly! And that is the decision she should make. But she is certain to try to get the project manager to commit to a lower number, and, if you do, then you only set up yourself—and her—to take a big fall later on.

It is your *obligation* to give the sponsor a valid cost so that she can make a valid decision about whether or not the project should be done. If you allow yourself to be intimidated into committing to a lower number, it is just going to be a disaster later on, and you are far better off taking your lumps now than being hanged later on.

Of course, there is another possibility. If she says she can afford only so much for the job, then you can offer to reduce the scope. If the job is viable at that scope level, then the project can be done. Otherwise, it is prudent to forget this project and do something else that can make profits for the company. As someone has said, there is a higher probability that things will accidentally go wrong in a project than that they will accidently go right. In terms of cost estimates, this means that there is always a higher likelihood that the budget will be overrun than that the project will come in below budget. This is just another way of stating Murphy's law, that "whatever can go wrong will go wrong."

> **There is a higher probability that things will accidentally go wrong in a project than that they will accidentally go right.**

The Phases of a Project

There are many different models for the phases a project goes through during its life cycle. One of these captures the all-too-frequent nature of projects that are not managed well and is shown in Figure 1-2.

I have shown this diagram to people all over the world, and they invariably laugh and say, "Yes, that's the way it works."

Figure 1-2. Life cycle of a troubled project.

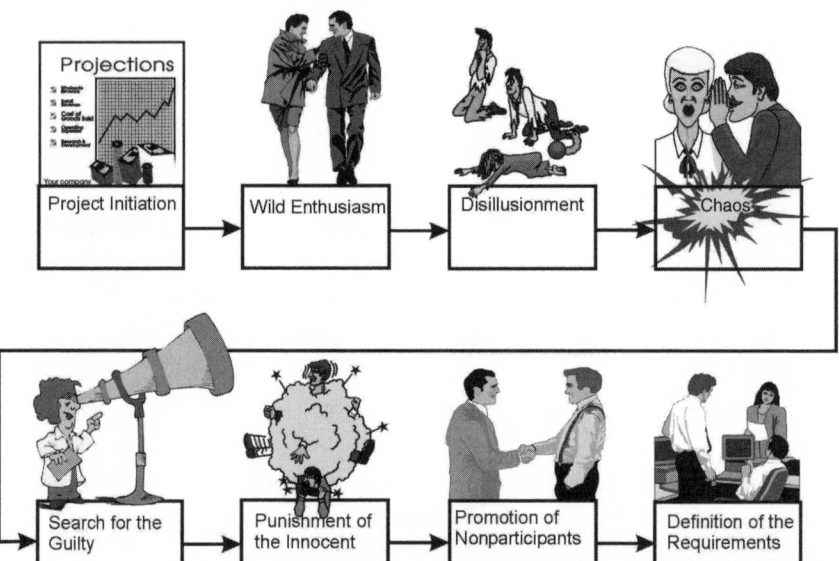

I suppose the comfort I can take is that we Americans are not the only ones who have the problem, but the bad news is that there are a lot of dysfunctional projects if everyone recognizes the model.

At the simplest level, a project has a beginning, middle, and end. I prefer the life-cycle model shown in Figure 1-3, but there are other versions that are equally valid. In my model, you will notice that every project begins as a concept, which is always "fuzzy," and that the project team must formalize the definition of the job before doing any work. However, because of our ready-fire-aim mentality, we often start working on the job without ensuring that we have a proper definition or that the mission and vision for the job are shared by everyone. This invariably leads to major problems as the project progresses. This is illustrated by the example that follows.

Definition Phase

Some years ago, a project manager in one of my client companies called me and said, "I've just had a conference call with key members of my project team, and I realized that we don't agree on what the project is supposed to accomplish."

I assured him that this was common.

"What should I do?" he asked.

I told him that he had no choice but to get the team members

Figure 1-3. Appropriate project life cycle.

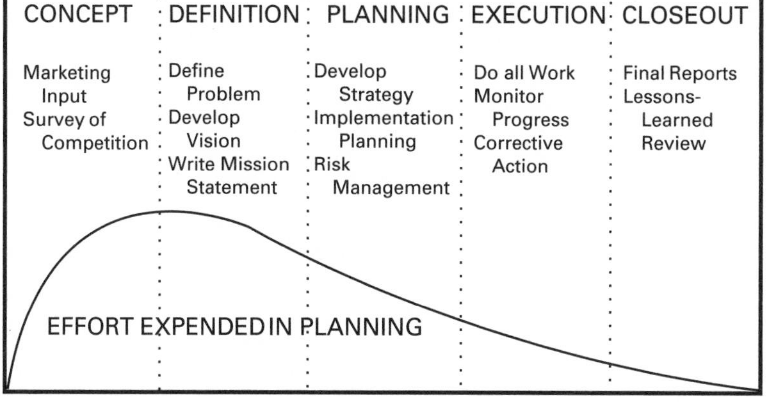

CONCEPT	DEFINITION	PLANNING	EXECUTION	CLOSEOUT
Marketing Input Survey of Competition	Define Problem Develop Vision Write Mission Statement	Develop Strategy Implementation Planning Risk Management	Do all Work Monitor Progress Corrective Action	Final Reports Lessons-Learned Review

EFFORT EXPENDED IN PLANNING

all going in the same direction by clarifying the mission of the project. He asked me to facilitate a meeting to do this.

At the meeting, I stood in front of a flip chart and began by saying, "Let's write a problem statement." Someone immediately countered by saying, "We don't need to do that. We all know what the problem is."

I was unmoved by this comment. I said, "Well, if that is true, it's just a formality and will only take a few minutes, and it would help me if we wrote it down, so someone help me get started."

I'm going to be a little facetious to illustrate what happened next. Someone said, "The," and I wrote the word on the chart, and someone else said, "I don't agree with that!"

Three hours later, we finally finished writing a problem statement.

The project manager was right. The team did not agree on what the problem was, much less how to solve it. This is fundamental—and is so often true that I begin to think we have a defective gene in all of us that prohibits us from insisting that we have a good definition of the problem before we start the work. Remember, project management is solving a problem on a large scale, and the way you define a problem determines how you will solve it. If you have the wrong definition, you may come up with the right solution—to the wrong problem!

In fact, I have become convinced that projects seldom fail at the end. Rather, they fail at the definition stage. I call these projects *headless-chicken projects* because they are like the chicken that has had its head chopped off and runs around spewing blood everywhere before it finally falls over and is "officially" dead. Projects work the same way. They spew blood all over the place, until someone finally says, "I think that project is dead," and indeed it is. But it was actually dead when we chopped off its head in the beginning—it just took a while for everyone to realize it.

Once the project is defined, you can plan how to do the work. There are three components to the plan: strategy, tactics, and logistics. Strategy is the overall approach or "game plan" that will be followed to do the work. An example of strategy was related to me by a friend who is into military history.

Strategy

During World War II, defense contractors were under great pressure to build weaponry at an intense level. To accelerate construction of ships and planes in particular, many new assembly methods were invented. Avondale shipyards, for example, worked on the method of building ships. The traditional way had always been to build the ship in an upright position. However, ships built from steel required welding in the bottom, or keel area of the boat, and this was very difficult to do. Avondale decided to build its ships upside down, to make the welding easier, and then turn them over to complete the structures above the top deck. This strategy was so effective that Avondale could build boats faster, cheaper, and of higher quality than their competitors, and the strategy is still being used today, nearly seventy years later.

Implementation Planning

This phase includes tactics and logistics. If you are going to build boats upside down, you must work out the details of how it will be done. A fixture must be constructed that will hold the boat and allow it to be turned over without being damaged. This is called "working out the tactics." It also includes the sequence in which the work will be done, who will do what, and how long each step will take.

Logistics deal with making sure the team has the materials and other supplies needed to do their jobs. Ordinarily we think about providing teams with the raw materials they need, but if the project is in a location where they can't get food, work will soon come to a grinding halt. So provisions must be made for the team to be fed—and possibly housed.

Execution and Control

Once the plan has been developed and approved, the team can begin work. This is the *execution* phase, but it also includes control, because, while the plan is being implemented, progress is monitored to ensure that the work is progressing according to the plan. When deviations from the plan occur, corrective action is taken to get the project back on track, or, if this is not possible, the plan is changed and approved, and the revised plan becomes the new baseline against which progress is tracked.

Closeout

When all the work has been completed, the *closeout* phase requires that a review of the project be conducted. The purpose is to learn lessons from this job that can be applied to future ones. Two questions are asked: "What did we do well?" and "What do we want to improve next time?"

Notice that we don't ask what was done wrong. This question tends to make people defensive, and they try to hide things that may result in their being punished. In fact, a lessons-learned review should never be conducted in a blame-and-punishment mode. If you are trying to conduct an inquisition, that's different. The purpose of an inquisition is usually to find who is responsible for major disasters and punish them. Lessons-learned sessions should be exactly what the words imply.

I have learned during the past few years that very few organizations do regular lessons-learned reviews of their projects. There is a reluctance to "open a can of worms." And there is a desire to get on with the next job. The problem is that you are almost sure to repeat the mistakes made on the previous project if no one knows about them or has an understanding of how they happened so that they can determine how to prevent them. But, perhaps most important, you can't even take advantage of the good things you did if you don't know about them.

It has been said that the organizations that survive and thrive in the future will be those that learn faster than their competitors. This seems especially true for projects.

The Steps in Managing a Project

The actual steps to manage a project are straightforward. Accomplishing them may not be. The model in Figure 1-4 illustrates the steps.

Figure 1-4. The steps in managing a project.

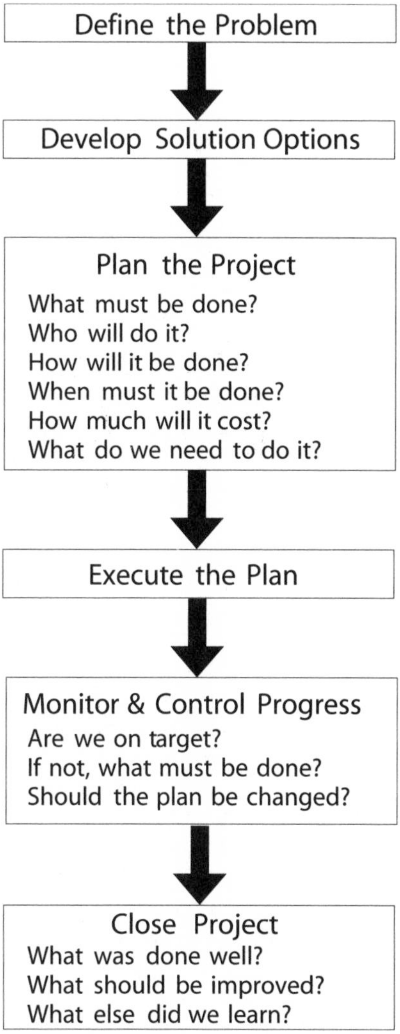

Define the Problem

↓

Develop Solution Options

↓

Plan the Project

What must be done?
Who will do it?
How will it be done?
When must it be done?
How much will it cost?
What do we need to do it?

↓

Execute the Plan

↓

Monitor & Control Progress
Are we on target?
If not, what must be done?
Should the plan be changed?

↓

Close Project
What was done well?
What should be improved?
What else did we learn?

Subsequent chapters of this book elaborate on how each step is accomplished. For now, here is a brief description of the actions involved.

Define the Problem

As was discussed previously, you need to identify the problem to be solved by the project. It helps to visualize the desired end result. What will be different? What will you see, hear, taste, touch, or smell? (Use sensory evidence if things can't be quantified.) What client need is being satisfied by the project?

Develop Solution Options

How many different ways might you go about solving the problem? Brainstorm solution alternatives (you can do this alone or as a group). Of the available alternatives, which do you think will best solve the problem? Is it more or less costly than other suitable choices? Will it result in a complete or only a partial fix?

Plan the Project

Planning is answering questions: what must be done, by whom, for how much, how, when, and so on. Naturally, answering these questions often requires a crystal ball. We discuss these steps in more detail in Chapters 2 through 4.

Execute the Plan

Obvious. Once the plan is drafted, it must be implemented. Interestingly, we sometimes find people going to great effort to put together a plan, then failing to follow it. If a plan is not followed, there is not much point in planning, is there?

Monitor and Control Progress

Plans are developed so that you can achieve your end result successfully. Unless progress is monitored, you cannot be sure you will succeed. It would be like having a roadmap to a destination but not monitoring the highway signs along the way.

Of course, if a deviation from the plan is discovered, you must ask what must be done to get back on track, or—if that seems impossible—how the plan should be modified to reflect new realities.

Close the Project

Once the destination has been reached, the project is finished, but there is a final step that should be taken. Some people call it an audit, others a postmortem (sounds a bit morbid, doesn't it?). Whatever you call it, the point is to learn something from what you just did. Note the way the questions are phrased: What was done well? What should be improved? What else did we learn? We can always improve on what we have done. However, asking "What did we do wrong?" is likely to make people a bit defensive, so the focus should be on improvement, not on placing blame. More on this later.

The Project Management Body of Knowledge (PMBOK®)

The Project Management Institute has attempted to determine a minimum body of knowledge that is needed by a project manager in order for him or her to be effective. As I mentioned earlier when I defined project management, there are five processes defined by the *PMBOK® Guide*, together with nine general areas of knowledge, and I will give brief summaries of them. If you want a complete document, you can get one by visiting the PMI website: *www.pmi.org*.

Project Processes

A *process* is a way of doing something. As previously mentioned, the *PMBOK® Guide* identifies five processes that are used to manage projects. Although some of them will be predominant at certain phases of a project, they may come into play at any time. Broadly speaking, however, they tend to be employed in the sequence listed as the project progresses. That is, initiating is done first, then planning, then executing, and so on. In the event that a project goes off course, replanning comes into play, and if a project is found to be in serious trouble, it may have to go all the way back to the initiating process to be restarted.

Initiating

Once a decision has been made to do a project, it must be *initiated* or launched. There are a number of activities associated with this. One is for the project sponsor to create a project charter, which defines what is to be done to meet the requirements of project customers. This is a formal process that is often omitted in organizations. The charter should be used to authorize work on the project; define the authority, responsibility, and accountability of the project team; and establish scope boundaries for the job. When such a document is not produced, the team members may misinterpret what is required of them, and this can be very costly.

Planning

One of the major causes of project failures is poor *planning*. Actually, I am being kind. Most of the time the problem is caused by there being no planning! The team simply tries to "wing it," to do the work without doing any planning at all. As I have explained earlier in this chapter, many of us are task oriented, and we see planning as a waste of time, so we would rather just get on with the work. As we will see when we turn to controlling the project, failing to develop a plan means that there can be no actual control of the project. We are just kidding ourselves.

Executing

There are two aspects to the process of project *execution*. One is to execute the work that must be done to create the product of the project. This is properly called technical work, and a project is conducted to produce a product. Note that we are using the word "product" in a very broad sense. A product can be an actual tangible piece of hardware or a building. It can also be software or a service of some kind. It can also be a result—consider, for example a project to service an automobile that consists of changing the oil and rotating the tires. There is no tangible deliverable for such a project, but there is clearly a result that must be achieved, and if it is not done correctly the car may be damaged as a result.

Executing also refers to implementing the project plan. It is amazing to find that teams often spend time planning a project, then abandon the plan as soon as they encounter some difficulty. Once they do this, they cannot have control of the work, since without a plan there is no control. The key is to either take corrective action to get back on track with the original plan or to revise the plan to show where the project is at present and continue forward from that point.

Monitoring and Controlling

Monitoring and *controlling* can actually be thought of as two separate processes, but because they go hand in hand, they are considered one activity. Control is exercised by comparing where project work is to where it is supposed to be, then taking action to correct for any deviations from target. Now the plan tells where the work should be. Without a plan, you don't know where you should be, so control is impossible, by definition.

Furthermore, knowing where you are is done by monitoring progress. An assessment of quantity and quality of work is made using whatever tools are available for the kind of work being done. The result of this assessment is compared to the planned level of work; if the actual level is ahead or behind of the plan, something will be done to bring progress back in line with the plan. Naturally, small deviations are always present and are ignored unless they exceed some pre-established threshold or show a trend toward drifting further off course.

Closing

In too many cases, once the product is produced to the customer's satisfaction, the project is considered finished, or *closed*. This should not be the case. A final lessons-learned review should be done before the project is considered complete. Failing to do a lessons-learned review means that future projects will likely suffer the same headaches encountered on the one just done.

Knowledge Areas

As previously mentioned, the *PMBOK® Guide* identifies nine knowledge areas that project managers should be familiar with in order to be considered professionals. These are as follows.

Project Integration Management

Project integration management ensures that the project is properly planned, executed, and controlled, including the exercise of formal project change control. As the term implies, every activity must be coordinated or integrated with every other one in order to achieve the desired project outcomes.

Project Scope Management

Changes to project scope are often the factors that kill a project. *Project scope management* includes authorizing the job, developing a scope statement that will define the boundaries of the project, subdividing the work into manageable components with deliverables, verifying that the amount of work planned has been achieved, and specifying scope change control procedures.

Project Time Management

I consider this a bad choice of terms, as "time management" implies personal efforts to manage one's time. *Project time management* specifically refers to developing a schedule that can be met, then controlling work to ensure that this happens! It's that simple. Because everyone refers to this as scheduling, it should really be called *schedule management.* (I know, I may be booted out of PMI for such heresy!)

Project Cost Management

This is exactly what it sounds like. *Project cost management* involves estimating the cost of resources, including people, equipment, materials, and such things as travel and other support details. After this is done, costs are budgeted and tracked to keep the project within that budget.

Project Quality Management

As I have commented earlier, one cause of project failure is that quality is overlooked or sacrificed so that a tight deadline can be met. It is not very helpful to complete a project on time, only to discover that the thing delivered won't work properly! *Project quality management* includes both quality assurance (planning to meet quality requirements) and quality control (steps taken to monitor results to see if they conform to requirements).

Project Human Resources Management

Project human resources management, often overlooked in projects, involves identifying the people needed to do the job; defining their roles, responsibilities, and reporting relationships; acquiring those people; and then managing them as the project is executed. Note that this topic does not refer to the actual day-to-day managing of people. The *PMBOK® Guide* mentions that these skills are necessary but does not attempt to document them. Given that these are the most important skills that a project manager must have, the *PMBOK® Guide* is deficient in omitting them.

Project Communications Management

As the title implies, *project communications management* involves planning, executing, and controlling the acquisition and dissemination of all information relevant to the needs of all project stakeholders. This information might include project status, accomplishments, and events that may affect other stakeholders or projects. Again, this topic does not deal with the actual process of communicating with someone. This topic is also mentioned but not included in the *PMBOK® Guide.*

Project Risk Management

Project risk management is the systematic process of identifying, quantifying, analyzing, and responding to project risk. It includes maximizing the probability and consequences of positive events and minimizing the probability and consequences of adverse events to project objectives. This is an extremely important aspect of project management that sometimes is overlooked by novice project managers.

Project Procurement Management

Procurement of necessary goods and services for the project is the logistics aspect of managing a job. *Project procurement management* involves deciding what must be procured, issuing requests for bids or quotations, selecting vendors, administering contracts, and closing them when the job is finished.

• •
Key Points to Remember

▶ A project is a temporary endeavor undertaken to produce a unique product, service, or result.

▶ A project is also a problem scheduled for solution.

▶ Project management is application of knowledge, skills, tools, and techniques to project activities to meet project requirements. Project management is accomplished by applying the processes of initiating, planning, executing, monitoring and controlling, and closing.

▶ All projects are constrained by Performance, Time, Cost, and Scope requirements. Only three of these can have values assigned. The fourth must be determined by the project team.

▶ Projects tend to fail because the team does not take time to ensure that they have developed a proper definition of the problem being solved.

▶ The major phases of a project include concept, definition, planning, execution and control, and closeout.
• •

Questions for Review

1. Project management is not just:
   a. planning
   b. rework
   c. scheduling
   d. controlling

2. The problem with being a working project manager is that, in a conflict between working and managing:
   a. You don't know what priorities to set.
   b. Your boss will think you're slacking off.
   c. There will never be enough time to do both.
   d. The work will take precedence and managing will suffer.

3. The *PMBOK® Guide* refers to:
   a. The body of knowledge identified by PMI as needed by project managers to be effective.
   b. A test administered by PMI to certify project managers
   c. An acronym for a special kind of risk analysis, like FMEA (Failure Mode and Effects Analysis)
   d. None of the above

4. Project scope defines:
   a. A project manager's visibility to the end date.
   b. The magnitude or size of the job.
   c. How often a project has been changed.
   d. The limits of a project manager's authority.

CHAPTER 2

The Role of the Project Manager

T he role of project managers seems to be very misunderstood throughout the world. Because many project managers arrive at their position as a natural progression from their jobs as engineers, programmers, scientists, and other kinds of jobs, both they and their bosses see the job as a technical job. This simply isn't true.

If you remember that every project produces a product, service, or result, then there is a technical aspect to the job. However, it is a question of who is responsible for what, and project managers who must manage the project and handle technical issues are set up to fail from the beginning. I will explain this later on. For now, suffice it to say that the primary responsibility of the project manager is to ensure that all work is completed on time, within budget and scope, and at the correct performance level. That is,

The primary responsibility of the project manager is to ensure that all work is completed on time, within budget and scope, and at the correct performance level.

she must see that the PCTS targets are met. Her primary role is to manage the project, not do the work!

What Is Managing?

The PMI definition of project management does not completely capture the true nature of project management. Remember, it says that "project management is application of knowledge, skills, tools, and techniques to project activities to meet the project requirements. Project management is accomplished through the application and integration of the 42 logically grouped project management processes comprising the 5 Process Groups: initiating, planning, executing, monitoring and controlling, and closing" (*PMBOK® Guide*, Project Management Institute, 2008, p. 6). That sounds nice on paper, but what is it that a person really does when he manages?

I don't know if it is really possible to convey what managing actually is. One reason is that project management is a *performing art*, and it is difficult to convey in words what an actor, athlete, or artist does. However, we can describe the various roles of a project manager, and that is the focus of this chapter. What should be clear is that you can't very well become something if you can't describe and define it, so this is a necessary exercise.

Definitions of Management

One common definition of management says that a manager gets work done by other people. Only a bit of thought is needed to realize how useless this definition is. Dictators get work done by other people, but I wouldn't call that management. Dr. Peter Drucker, whom many credit with being the "father" of management because he first made people realize that management was a profession, rather than a job, has said that a manager is supposed to make an unsolicited contribution to the organization. That is, a manager looks around to see what needs to be done to advance the cause of the organization and does it without asking permission or having to be told to do it. This is often called being proactive, as opposed to reactive, and it is.

But, most important, a manager can't do this unless she understands the mission and vision for the organization and takes initiative to help achieve these. And I believe this applies equally well to project managers. First, they must understand the mission and vision of the organization; then they must see how the project they are managing meshes with the organization's mission; then they must steer the project to ensure that the interests of the organization are met.

> **Project managers must understand the mission and vision of the organization first, then they must see how the project they are managing meshes with the organization's mission, and they must steer the project to ensure that the interests of the organization are met.**

It's about People!

In addition, I said earlier that the job is not a technical job. It is about getting people to perform work that must be done to meet the objectives of the project. In that respect, the classical definition is correct, but Drucker has pointed out that the manager must get people to perform above the minimum acceptable performance level. The reason is that this minimum level is the survival level for the organization, and any company that just manages to survive will not do so for long. Eventually the competition will pass it by, and the organization will die.

So the first skills that a project manager needs are *people skills*. Herein lies the source of major problems for many project managers—and general managers, too, for that matter. I have found that most managers know more about getting performance from computers, machines, and money than they do about getting people to perform. There are many reasons for this, but chief among them is that nobody has ever taught them practical methods for dealing with people, and we simply aren't born knowing how. So far as I know, the geneticists have not yet found a people-skills gene that endows a person with these skills.

Furthermore, many project managers who have strong technical backgrounds find it difficult to deal with people effectively. They are "things oriented," not people oriented, and some will even go so far as to say that they hate this aspect of the job. My recommendation is that they forget about being project managers if this is true. You usually aren't very effective at something you hate doing, but, beyond that, why spend your life doing something you hate?

The Working Project Manager

In fact, one of the biggest traps for project managers is to be what is euphemistically called a *working project manager*. This means that the project manager is indeed responsible for performing technical work, in addition to managing the job. The problem with this is that when there is a conflict between managing and doing work—and there always is such a conflict—the work will take priority and the managing will be neglected. However, when it comes time for the manager's performance appraisal, he will be told that his technical work was okay, but the managing was inadequate. This is a double bind that should not exist.

Authority

The universal complaint from project managers is that they have a lot of responsibility but no authority. It is true, and it is not likely to change. It is the nature of the job, I'm afraid. However, you can't delegate responsibility without giving a person the authority commensurate with the responsibility you want him to take, so, while the project manager's authority might be limited, it cannot be zero.

A word to project managers, however. I learned early in my career as an engineer that you have as much authority as you are willing to take. I know that sounds strange. We see authority as something granted to us by the organization, but it turns out that those individuals who take authority for granted usually get it officially. Of course, I am not advocating that you violate any of the policies of the organization. That is not a proper use of authority. But when it comes to making decisions, rather than checking with your boss to see if something is okay, make the decision yourself, take action that is appropriate and does not violate policy, and then inform your boss what you have done. Many managers have told me that they wish their people would quit placing all decisions on their shoulders to make. And they wish their people would bring them solutions, rather than problems. In other words, your boss is looking for you to take some of the load and leave her free to do other things.

A Moment of Truth

Jan Carlzon was the youngest ever CEO of Scandinavian Airlines, and he successfully turned around the ailing airline. He did so in part by empowering all employees to do their jobs without having to ask permission for every action they felt they should take to meet customer needs. He pointed out that every interaction between an employee and a customer was a *moment of truth* in which the customer would evaluate the airline's service. If that service was good, then the customer would be likely to fly SAS again; conversely, if it wasn't good, the customer would be less likely to do so. As Carlzon pointed out, from the customer's point of view, the SAS employee *is* the airline.

Furthermore, Carlzon revised the standard organization chart, which is typically a triangle with the CEO at the apex and successive levels of managers cascading down below, eventuating to the front-line employees at the very bottom. This implies that there is more and more authority as you go from the bottom toward the apex at the top and that the people at the lowest level have almost no authority at all.

Carlzon simply inverted the triangle, placing the apex at the bottom and the front-line employees at the top. In doing so, he said that the job of managers is to make it possible for the front line to deliver the services that the customer expects. The manager is an *enabler* of employees. They are actually servants of employees, not their masters, when you look at it this way.

This is, to me, the essence of the project manager's role. Since you have very little authority anyway, consider that your job is to ensure that everyone in the project team has what he needs to do his job well. If you do, then most of your team will perform at appropriate levels.

> **Since you have very little authority anyway, consider the job to ensure that everyone in the project team has what they need to do their job well.**

Leadership and Management

Finally, because the project manager's job is mostly about dealing with people, it is absolutely essential that you exercise leadership as well as management skills (see Chapter 13). I have defined management as making an unsolicited contribution to the organization. The definition of leadership that seems to me to best express the meaning of the word is this (from *The Pyramid Climbers*): "Leadership is the art of getting others to *want* to do something that you believe should be done." The operative word in the definition is "want."

As I said previously, dictators get people to do things. Leaders get them to *want* to do things. There is a big difference. As soon as the dictator turns her back, people quit working. When the leader turns her back, people continue working, because they are working willingly.

Clearly, a project manager needs to exercise leadership, since he lacks authority. But, most important, the dictator can control only those people within his immediate range of sight. The leader can get people to perform without having to closely supervise them. And this is necessary in projects.

However, a project manager must also exercise management

skills. In fact, the two sets of skills must be integrated into the job of project management because management deals with the administrated aspects of the job—budgets, schedules, logistics, and so on—while leadership gets people to perform at optimum levels. If you exercise one set of skills to the exclusion of the other, the outcome will be far less effective than if you integrate the two skill sets.

Do You Want to Be a Project Manager?

Project management is not for everyone. I emphasized earlier that it is not a technical job. It is about getting people to perform work that must be done to meet the objectives of the project. So when I am asked what I consider to be the most important attributes for project managers to have, I always say that people skills are number one through three. Then, below that, comes everything else. If you can deal with people, you can either learn to do everything else or delegate it to someone who can do it. But being able to do everything else without being good at dealing with people just won't cut it.

> So when I am asked what I consider to be the most important attributes for project managers to have, I always say that people skills are number one through three.

Now the question is, do you really want to be a project manager? Do you like having responsibility with very limited authority? Do you enjoy working to impossible deadlines, with limited resources and unforgiving stakeholders? Are you, in other words, a bit masochistic? If you are, then you will love being a project manager.

If you are the boss of project managers, these are things you should consider in selecting people for the job. Not everyone is cut out for the job.

Key Points to Remember

▶ A project manager must understand the mission and vision of the organization first, see how the project they are managing meshes with the organization's mission, and then steer the project to ensure that the interests of the organization are met.

▶ The first skills a project manager needs are people skills.

▶ One of the biggest traps for project managers is to perform technical work in addition to managing the job, because, when there is a conflict between performing the two, the project manager cannot neglect the management aspects.

▶ Instead of asking for authority, make decisions yourself, take action that is appropriate and does not violate policy, and then inform your boss what you have done.

▶ The project manager's job is to ensure that everyone in the project team has what he needs to do his job well.

▶ A project manager must exercise both leadership and management skills.

CHAPTER 3

Planning the Project

n Chapter 1, I talked about the high cost of project failures. Almost every study finds that failures are caused primarily by poor project management, especially the failure to plan properly. There are two barriers to good planning. The first is prevailing paradigms, and the second is the nature of human beings.

A paradigm is a belief about what the world is like. You can tell what people believe by watching what they do, because they always behave consistently with their deeply held beliefs. It is not necessarily what they say they believe but what they *really* believe that counts. Chris Argyris, in his book *Overcoming Organizational Defenses: Facilitating Organization Learning*, has called these beliefs one's *theory espoused* as opposed to one's *theory in practice*. To illustrate, a fellow who attended my seminar on the tools of project management later told me that, upon returning to work, he immediately convened a meeting of his project team to prepare a plan. His boss called him out of the conference room.

"What are you doing?" asked the boss.

"Planning our project," explained the fellow.

"Oh, you don't have time for that nonsense," his boss told him. "Get them out of the conference room so they can get the job done!"

It is clear that his boss didn't believe in planning, which raises this question: Why did he send the fellow to a training program if he really didn't believe in what is taught? Go figure.

The second reason that people don't plan is that they find the activity painful. Some individuals, especially engineers and programmers, are concerned that they will be held to estimates of task durations that they have made using their best guesses. Because they have no historical data to draw on, this is all they can do. But they also know that such numbers are highly uncertain, and they are afraid that failure to meet established targets will get them in trouble. As one of my engineers told me once, "You can't schedule creativity."

I replied that this may be true, but we must pretend we can, because no one will fund the project unless we put down a time. Since then, I have changed my mind—you can schedule creativity, within limits. In fact, there is no better stimulus to creative thinking than a tight deadline. If you give people forever, they simply mess around and don't produce anything.

Nevertheless, we find that, when people are required to plan a project, they find the activity painful, and they resist the pain it causes. The net result is that they wind up on the pain curve numbered 1 in Figure 3-1. The net result of being on this curve is to experience a lot of pain, because the total pain experienced is represented by the area under the curve.

In curve 2 of the figure, there is a lot of pain early on, but it diminishes over time, and the total area under the curve is less than that under curve 1.

The Absolute Imperative of Planning

If you consider the major function of managing, it is to ensure that desired organization objectives are met. This is accomplished by exercising control over scarce resources. However, the word

Figure 3-1. Two pain curves in a project over time.

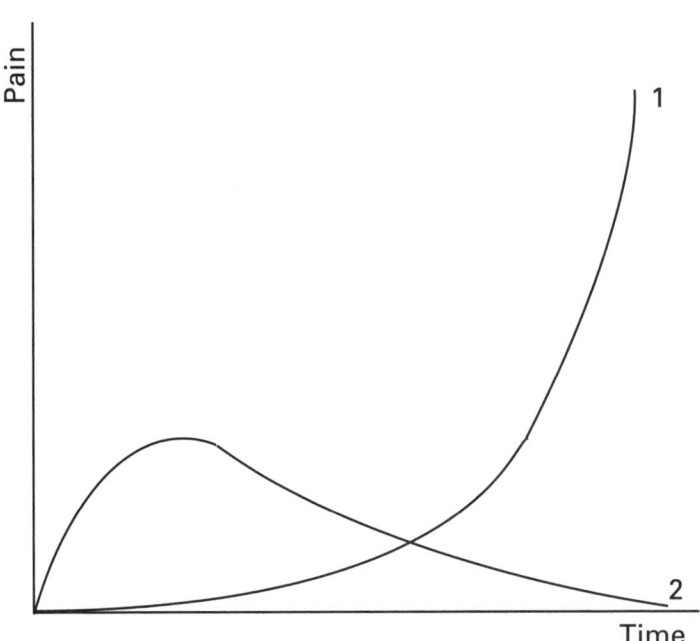

control has two connotations, and we must be careful which one we intend.

One meaning of the word is "power and domination." In management, this is sometimes called the command-and-control approach, which in its worst form degenerates into the use of fear and intimidation to get things done. This method works when people have no other desirable options for employment or are not free to leave (as in the military or a prison). However, in a robust economy, very few employees tolerate such management for long.

The second meaning of control—and the one I advocate for managers—is highlighted in the idea that control is exer-

> **Control is exercised by comparing where you are to where you are supposed to be so that corrective action can be taken when there is a deviation.**

cised by comparing where you are to where you are supposed to be so that corrective action can be taken when there is a deviation. Notice that this is an information systems or guidance definition. Furthermore, note that two things are necessary for control to exist. First, you must have a plan that tells where you are supposed to be in the first place. If you have no plan, then, you cannot possibly have control. I think we need to remind ourselves of this almost every day, because it is so easy to forget when you are constantly being assaulted by demands to do this and that and a million other things.

> **No plan, no control!**

Second, if you don't know where you are, you can't have control. Knowing where you are isn't as easy as it may seem, especially in doing knowledge work. For example, you say you expect to write ten thousand lines of code by today, and you've written eight thousand. Does that mean you're 80 percent of where you should be? Not necessarily. You may have found a more efficient way to write the code.

> **Predicting the future is easy. It's knowing what's going on now that's hard.**
>
> —Fritz R. S. Dressler

In any event, the major point to remember is that you cannot have control unless you have a plan, so planning is not optional.

Another trap that causes people not to plan is to believe that they have no time to plan; they need to get the job done really fast! This is counterintuitive, but think about it—if you have forever to get something done, then you don't need a plan. It's when the deadline is tight that the plan becomes really important. As a simple example, imagine flying into Chicago and being late. You have a meeting across town in less than an hour. You've never been to Chicago, but when the rental car attendant asks if you need a map, you say, "I don't have time for a map. I've got to get to my meeting really fast!" Not very likely, is it?

Planning Defined

Planning is quite simply answering the questions shown in Figure 3-2. They may be called the "who, what, when, why, how much, how long?" questions that you learned if you ever studied interviewing methods. It is that simple. And it is that hard. I say hard because answering some of these questions requires a crystal ball—especially questions like "How long will that take?" On tasks for which no history is available, this is a very hard question to answer. As my engineer said, "You can't schedule creativity."

Figure 3-2. Planning is answering questions.

Strategy, Tactics, and Logistics

To plan a project properly, you must attend to three kinds of activities that may have to be performed during the life of the job. These are strategy, tactics, and logistics.

Strategy refers to the overall method you will employ to do the job, sometimes referred to as a "game plan." As I related in Chapter 1, for thousands of years boats have been built with the keel down so that when one wishes to put the boat in the water, it is already right side up. This method worked fine until the

1940s, when World War II placed tremendous pressure on shipyards to build military ships faster and ships were being built out of steel plate, rather than wood. Shipbuilders quickly found that it was extremely difficult to weld in the keel area. From the outside, you had problems getting under the ship, and inside you had to stand on your head to weld.

Avondale shipyards decided that it would be easier to build steel boats if ships were built upside down. The welding in the keel area now could be done from outside, standing above the ship, and to work on the inside one could stand upright. This strategy proved so effective that Avondale could build boats faster, cheaper, and of higher quality than its competitors, and the approach is still being used today.

Too often planners choose a project strategy because "it has always been done that way," rather than because it is best. You should always ask yourself, "What would be the best way to go about this?" before you proceed to do detailed implementation planning.

Implementation Planning

Once you have decided to build boats upside down, you must work out all of the details of how it will be done. Sometimes we say that we must be sure to dot all of the "i's" and cross all the "t's." This is where you answer those "who, what, when, and where" questions. In fact, it is implementation planning that many people think of when they talk about planning. However, a well-developed implementation plan for the wrong project strategy can only help you fail more efficiently.

Logistics

Military people can quickly tell you the benefit of attention to logistics. You can't fight a battle if people have no ammunition, food, clothing, or transportation. It is logistics that attends to these things. I once saw a project scheduling program (regrettably now defunct) that allowed construction managers to record when a certain quantity of bricks was delivered to their site; it then showed when they would run out, given a specific utilization rate. This would alert managers to schedule delivery of a new supply just before the existing stock was depleted.

I was also told about a road construction project in India that had very bad living conditions for the workers. The food was bad, sleeping conditions were poor, and the workers were suffering low morale. The project manager and his staff were all staying in a nice hotel in a nearby city. They finally realized the problem and moved to the site with the workers. Living conditions immediately improved, and so did worker morale. This is an example of the importance of a peripheral aspect of logistics.

Plan Ingredients

Following are the *minimum ingredients* that should be contained in a project plan. It is a good idea to keep these in a *centralized project database*. Initially, the *electronic file* will contain only the plan. As the project is managed, reports, changes, and other documents will be added, so that when the project is completed the *file* will contain a complete history of the project, which can be used by others as data for planning and managing their own projects.

Here are the items that make up the project plan:

▶ Problem statement.

▶ Project mission statement (see Chapter 4 for instructions on how to develop a mission statement).

▶ Project objectives (see discussion in Chapter 4).

▶ Project work requirements, including a list of all deliverables, such as reports, hardware, software, and so on. It is a good idea to have a deliverable at each major project milestone so that progress can be measured more easily.

▶ Exit criteria. Each milestone should have criteria established that will be used to determine whether the preceding phase of work is actually finished. If no deliverable is provided at a milestone, exit criteria become very important.

▶ End-item specifications to be met. This means engineering specifications, architectural specs, building codes, government regulations, and so on.

▶ Work breakdown structure (WBS). This is an identification of all of the tasks that must be performed in order to achieve project objectives. A WBS is also a good graphic portrayal of *project scope* (see Chapter 6).

▶ Schedules (both milestone and working schedules should be provided; see Chapters 7 and 8).

▶ Required resources (people, equipment, materials, and facilities). These must be specified in conjunction with the schedule (see Chapters 7 and 8).

▶ Control system (see Chapters 9, 10, and 11).

▶ Major contributors. Use a linear responsibility chart (see Chapter 6).

▶ Risk areas with contingencies when possible (see Chapters 4 and 5).

Sign-Off of the Plan

Once the plan has been prepared, it should be submitted to *stakeholders* for their signatures.

Following are some comments about the meaning of a signature and suggestions for handling the process:

▶ A signature means that the individual is *committed* to his contribution, agrees with the scope of work to be done, and accepts the specs as valid. A signature on the part of a contributor does not mean a *guarantee* of

STAKEHOLDER: Anyone who has a vested interest in the project. These include contributors, customers, managers, and financial people.

performance. It is a commitment. Because there are factors outside our control, few of us would like to guarantee our performance. However, most would be willing to make a commitment, meaning we promise to do our best to fulfill our obligations. If a signature is treated as a guarantee, either signers will refuse to sign or they will sign without feeling really committed to the agreement. Neither response is desirable.

> The plan should be signed in a *project plan review meeting*, not by mail. Circulating copies for signature by mail seldom works, as people may be too busy to read in depth and may miss important points that would be brought out in a signoff meeting.

The project plan should be reviewed and signed off in a meeting—not through interoffice mail!

> People should be encouraged to "shoot holes in the plan" during the review meeting, rather than wait until problems develop later on. Naturally, this does not mean that they should nitpick the plan. The objective is to ensure that the plan is workable—that is all.

Encourage people to spot problems during the sign-off meeting, not later.

Changing the Plan

It would be nice to think that a plan, once developed, would never change. However, that is unrealistic. No one has 20/20 foresight. Unforeseen problems are almost certain to arise. The important thing is to make changes in an orderly way, following a standard change procedure.

Make changes in an orderly way, following a standard change procedure.

If no change control is exercised, the project may wind up over budget, behind schedule, and hopelessly inadequate, with no warning until it is too late. Here are suggestions for handling changes to the plan:

▶ Changes should be made only when a significant deviation occurs. A significant change is usually specified in terms of percent tolerances relative to the original targets.

▶ Change control is necessary to protect *everyone* from the effects of scope creep—changes to the project that result in additional work. If changes in scope are not identified and managed properly, the project may come in considerably over budget and/or behind schedule.

> **Any plan is bad which is not susceptible to change.**
>
> —Bartolommno de San Concordio (1475–1517)

▶ Causes of changes should be documented for reference in planning future projects. The causes should be *factual*, not blame-and-punishment statements.

A comprehensive process for managing project change is presented in Chapter 10.

Suggestions for Effective Planning

Here are some ideas to help you plan effectively:

▶ Plan to plan. It is always difficult to get people together to develop a plan. The planning session itself should be planned, or it may turn into a totally disorganized meeting of the type that plagues many organizations. This means that an agenda must be prepared, the meeting should be time limited to the degree possible, and people should be kept on track. If someone goes off on a tangent, the meeting facilitator should get the person back on track as quickly as possible. There are many excellent guides to running meetings (e.g., *Mining Group Gold* by Tom Kayser); the reader is referred to those.

▶ The people who must implement a plan should participate in preparing it. Otherwise, you risk having contributors who feel no sense of commitment to the plan; their estimates may be erroneous, and major tasks may be forgotten.

> **Rule: The people who must do the work should participate in developing the plan.**

▶ The first rule of planning is to be prepared to replan. Unexpected obstacles will undoubtedly crop up and must be handled. This also means that you should not plan in too much detail if there is a likelihood that the plan will have to be changed, as this wastes time.

> **The first rule of planning is to be prepared to replan!**

▶ Because unexpected obstacles will crop up, always conduct a risk analysis to anticipate the most likely ones (see Chapter 5). Develop Plan B just in case Plan A doesn't work. Why not just use Plan B in the first place? Because Plan A is better but has a few weaknesses. Plan B has weaknesses also, but they must be different from those in Plan A, or there is no use in considering Plan B a backup.

The simple way to do a risk analysis is to ask, "What could go wrong?" This should be done for the schedule, work performance, and other parts of the project plan. Sometimes, simply identifying risks can help avert them, but, if that cannot be done, at least you'll have a backup plan available. One caution: If you are dealing with very analytical people, they may go into *analysis paralysis* here. You are not trying to identify *every possible risk*—just those that are fairly likely.

> **Identify project risks and develop contingencies to deal with them if they occur.**

▶ Begin by looking at the *purpose* of doing whatever is to be done. Develop a problem statement. All actions in an organization should be taken to achieve a result, which is another way of saying "solve a problem." Be careful here to identify what the end user really needs to solve the problem. Sometimes we see projects in which the team thinks a solution is right for the client, but that solution is never used, resulting in significant waste to the organization.

▶ Use the Work Breakdown Structure (discussed in Chapter 6) to divide the work into smaller chunks for which you can develop accurate estimates for duration, cost, and resource requirements.

> **Consider the little mouse, how sagacious an animal it is which never entrusts its life to one hole only.**
>
> —Plautus (254–184 B.C.)

Project Planning Steps

The basic planning steps are as follows. Note that some of these topics are covered in the next chapter.

▶ Define the problem to be solved by the project.

▶ Develop a mission statement, followed by statements of major objectives.

▶ Develop a project strategy that will meet all project objectives.

▶ Write a scope statement to define project boundaries (what *will* and *will not* be done).

> **Be sure the project really satisfies the customer's needs, rather than being what the team thinks the customer should get!**

▶ Develop a Work Breakdown Structure (WBS).

▶ Using the WBS, estimate activity durations, resource requirements, and costs (as appropriate for your environment).

▶ Prepare the project master schedule and budget.

▶ Decide on the project organization structure—whether matrix or hierarchical (if you are free to choose).

▶ Create the project plan.

▶ Get the plan signed off by all project stakeholders.

· ·
Key Points to Remember

▶ If you have no plan, you have no control.

▶ The people who must execute a plan should participate in preparing it.

▶ Have the plan signed off in a meeting, not by sending it through the interoffice mail.

▶ Keep all project documentation in an electronic project file.

▶ Use exit criteria to determine when a milestone has actually been achieved.

▶ Require that changes to the project plan be approved before you make them.

▶ Risk management should be part of all project planning.

▶ A paradigm is a belief about what the world is like.

▶ Planning is answering the "who, what, when, how, how long, and how much" questions.

▶ Logistics refers to supplying people with materials and supplies they need to do their jobs.
· ·

Exercise ·

We have talked about strategy, tactics, and logistics. Which must be decided first? What is the function of tactics? When would you plan for logistics?

CHAPTER 4

Developing a Mission, Vision, Goals, and Objectives for the Project

efore a project team does any work, it should spend time ensuring that it has a shared understanding of where it is going. The terms used to define that destination are "mission," "vision," "goals," and "objectives." And it is at this very early stage that projects tend to fail, because everyone takes for granted that "we all know what the mission is."

Defining the Problem

Every project solves a problem of some kind, but people are inclined to skip over the definition of the problem. This is a big mistake. The way you define a problem determines how you will solve it, so it is critical that a proper definition be developed. For example, too often a problem is defined in terms of a solution. A person may say, "I have a problem. My car has quit, and I have no way to get to work. How am I going to get my car repaired, because I have no money to do it?"

The problem has essentially been defined as "How do I repair my car?" The actual problem, however, at its most fundamental level, is that the person has no way to get to work—or so he says. But could he ride the bus, go with a coworker, or ride a bike until he has the money to have the car repaired? It is true that having no money to repair the car is a problem, but it is important to distinguish between the basic or core problem and those at another level.

I once heard a sales manager berate a salesman, saying, "The company has spent a lot of money developing this new product, and none of you are selling it. If you don't get out there and sell this product, I'm going to find myself some salespeople who can sell!"

It is clear how he has defined the problem—he has a group of salespeople who can't sell. However, given that none of them can sell the product, I am sure he is wrong. There is something wrong with the product or market, or the competition is killing them. You are very unlikely to have *all* bad salespeople!

> **A problem is a gap between where you are and where you want to be, with obstacles existing that prevent easy movement to close the gap.**

Nevertheless, this manager has defined the problem in terms of people, and that is the way it must be solved. Imagine that he replaces all of the salespeople. He will still have the same problem, because he has not addressed the actual cause.

People sometimes define a problem as a goal. A goal in itself is not a problem. It is when there are obstacles that make it difficult to reach the goal that one has a problem. Given this definition of a problem, we can say that problem solving involves finding ways to deal with obstacles: They must be overcome, bypassed, or removed.

Confusion of Terms

Suppose a person tells you that she is taking a new job in a distant city, and she plans to move there. She immediately realizes that she must find a place to live. So she says, "I have a problem. I have to find a place to live."

You ask her what her mission is. "To find a place to live," she says.

And how about her vision? "To have a place to live," she answers, a little confused.

No wonder she is confused. All three statements sound alike! She needs to understand the difference between them if she is to solve this problem.

Remember, a problem is a gap. Suppose we were to ask her to tell us where she wants to be when her problem is solved. She would say, "I would have a place to live in the new city."

"And where are you now?" you ask.

"I have no place to live," she says.

Then the gap is between having a place and not having one. This can be stated simply as "I have no place to live." And, indeed, this is the problem she is trying to solve.

But—would just *any* place be okay? Of course not. She doesn't want to live under a bridge, although homeless people sometimes do. So if you ask her, "What kind of place are you looking for?" she can tell you.

"It needs to have three bedrooms, the house must be of a certain size, and I prefer a certain style," she says. This is her vision for the kind of place she wants to live in. That vision literally paints a picture in her mind, and, when she finds a place that comes close to that picture, she will have "arrived" at her destination. This is the function of vision—it defines "done."

Her mission, then, is to find a place that conforms to her vision. Another way to say this is that the mission of a project is always to achieve the vision. In doing so, it solves the stated problem. So you may want to diagram it as shown in Figure 4-1. Note that the vision has been spelled out as a list of things she must have, along with some that she wants to have and a few that would be nice to have if she could get them.

**Figure 4-1. Chevron showing mission, vision,
and problem statement.**

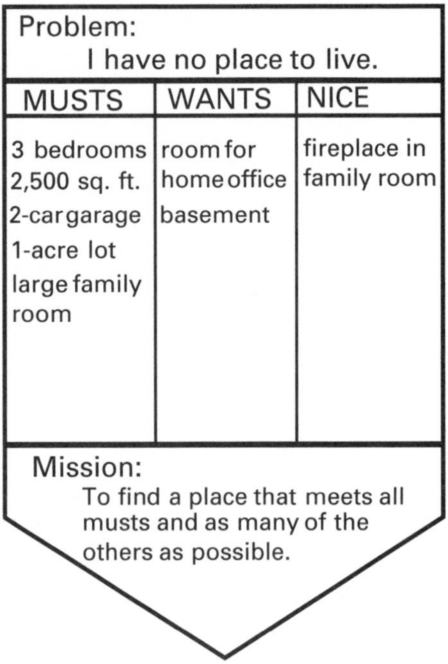

Problem: I have no place to live.		
MUSTS	WANTS	NICE
3 bedrooms 2,500 sq. ft. 2-car garage 1-acre lot large family room	room for home office basement	fireplace in family room

Mission:
To find a place that meets all
musts and as many of the
others as possible.

The Real World

Okay, now we know the differences among the mission, vision, and problem, but in the "real world" you never get them in this order. Your boss or project sponsor will say, "Here is your mission," without any mention of a problem statement. It is possible that some discussion of the sponsor's vision of the end result will take place, but even that may be fairly sketchy. So the first order of business for a project team is to develop these into a form that everyone will accept.

The major "political" problem you may encounter is that the sponsor will undoubtedly have given you a mission that is based on his definition of the problem to be solved. Sometimes his definition will be incorrect, and you will have to confront this. Otherwise, you will spend a lot of the organization's money, only to find that you have developed the right solution to the wrong problem.

The Real Mission of Every Project

I said earlier that the mission is always to achieve the vision. However, I should add that the vision you are trying to achieve is the one the customer holds. Another way to say this is that you are trying to satisfy the customer's needs. That is the primary objective. Your motive may be to make a profit in the process, but the mission is always to meet the needs of the customer. That means, of course, that you must know what those needs are, and sometimes this isn't easy, because even the customer isn't clear about them. So you have to translate or interpret as best you can. Your best safeguard is to keep the customer involved in the project from concept to completion so that there is a constant check on whether what you are doing will achieve the desired result.

The mission of the project can be written by answering two questions:

1. What are we going to do?

2. For whom are we going to do it?

In the previous edition of this book, it was suggested that you also state how you will go about meeting those customer needs, but this should not be part of the mission statement itself. The mission statement defines "what" you are doing; "how" you are going to do it is project strategy and should be dealt with separately.

Developing Project Objectives

Once a mission statement has been developed, you can write your project objectives. Note that objectives are much more specific than the mission statement itself and define results that must be achieved in order for the overall mission to be accomplished. Also, an objective defines the desired end result.

I may want to finish this chapter by 10 o'clock this morning. That is my desired outcome or result—my objective. The way in which I achieve that objective is to perform a number of tasks. These might include typing text into my computer, reviewing some other literature on the topic about which I am writing, calling a colleague to ask a question for clarification, and printing out the chapter, proofing it, and entering some revisions into my computer.

The following acronym may help you remember the essential qualities that a statement of objectives must have. We say that an objective must be SMART, each letter standing for a condition as follows:

> **Goal setting has traditionally been based on past performance. This practice has tended to perpetuate the sins of the past.**
>
> —J. M. Juran

Specific

Measurable

Attainable

Realistic

Time limited

Dr. W. Edwards Deming has raised some serious questions about the advisability of trying to quantify goals and objectives. He argued that there is no point in setting quotas for a manufacturing process to reach. If the system is stable, he argued, then there is no need to specify a goal, since you will get whatever the system can produce. A goal beyond the capability of the system can't be achieved.

> **An objective specifies a desired end result to be achieved. A task is an activity performed to achieve that result. An objective is usually a noun, whereas a task is a verb.**

On the other hand, according to Deming, if the system is not stable (in the statistical sense of the word), then again there is no need to specify a quota, since there is no way to know what the capability of the system is.

In project work, we may know the capability of a person by looking at his or her past performance, but, unless you have a large number of samples, you have no way of knowing exactly what the person can do, since there is always variability in people's performance. Furthermore, it does no good to base a quota on what someone else has done. The quota must be valid for the person who is going to do the job this time.

We all know that some people are capable of more output than others. So defining the measurement and attainability aspects of goal or objective setting is very difficult. I go into this more in Chapter 6 when I discuss time estimating.

I have found the following two questions to be useful both in setting objectives and in monitoring progress toward those objectives:

1. What is our desired outcome? This is called the outcome frame. It helps keep you focused on the result you are trying to achieve, rather than on the effort being expended to get there.

2. How will we know when we achieve it? I call this the evidence question. This question is very useful for establishing exit criteria for objectives that cannot be quantified.

What follows are a couple of examples of objectives:

▶ Our objective is to develop a one-minute commercial to solicit contributions to WXYZ to air on local TV stations by June 5, 2012.

▶ Our objective is to raise $600,000 in funds from local viewers by September 18, 2012.

The Nature of Objectives

Note that these examples of objectives do not say how they will be achieved. I consider an objective to be a statement that tells me what result is to be achieved. The "how" is problem solving, and I prefer to keep that open so that solutions can be brainstormed later. If the approach is written into the objective statement, it may lock a team into a method that is not really best for the project.

Assessing Project Risks

Once you have established your objectives, you can develop plans for how to achieve them. Unfortunately, the best plans sometimes don't work. One safeguard in managing projects is to think about the risks ahead that could sink the job. This can be done for critical objectives and for other parts of the plan.

The simplest way to conduct a risk analysis is to ask, "What could go wrong?" or "What could keep us from achieving our objective?" It is usually best to list the risks first, then think about contingencies for dealing with them. One way to look at risk is to divide a flip chart page in half, have the group brainstorm the risks, which you write down on the left side of the page, and then go back and list the contingencies—things you can do to manage the risks if they do materialize. An example of a risk analysis for a photography project is shown in Figure 4-2.

One benefit of doing a risk analysis in this manner is that it may help you avert some risks. When you cannot avert a risk, you will at least have a backup plan. Unexpected risks can throw a project into a tailspin.

> **It is helpful to assess risks of failure of the following:**
> - ▶ **The schedule**
> - ▶ **The budget**
> - ▶ **Project quality**
> - ▶ **Customer satisfaction**

Figure 4-2. Risk analysis example.

What could go wrong?	Contingency
1. Exposure wrong	Bracket the exposure
2. Shots unacceptable	Take extra photos
3. Film lost or damaged	Hand carry to client
4. Weather delays	Allow extra time

I mentioned this point previously, but it bears repeating: You are not trying to identify every possible risk, just some of the more likely ones. This point should be made to team members who are highly analytical or who perhaps have a tendency to be negative in general. Also, risk analysis always has a positive thrust—that is, you are asking, "If it happens, what will we do about it?" You don't want people to say, "Ain't it awful!"

Risk analysis should not lead to analysis paralysis!

In Chapter 5, I present detailed tools and techniques to address risk management in the project environment.

Key Points to Remember

▶ The way a problem is defined determines how you will solve it.

▶ A problem is a gap between where you are and where you want to be, with obstacles making it hard to reach the goal. A goal by itself is not a problem. Obstacles must exist for there to be a problem.

▶ Vision is what the final result will "look like." It defines "done."

▶ The mission is to achieve the vision. It answers the two questions "What are we going to do?" and "For whom are we going to do it?"

▶ Objectives should be SMART.

▶ You can identify risks by asking, "What could go wrong?"

Exercise

Choose a project that you are going to do or perhaps have just started. Answer the questions that follow to the best of your ability. If you need to confer with others to answer some of them, fine. Remember, the people who have to follow the plan should participate in preparing it.

▶ What are you trying to achieve with the project? What need does it satisfy for your customer? Who exactly is going to actually use the project deliverable(s) when it is finished? (That is, who is your real customer?) What will distinguish your deliverable from those already available to the customer?

▶ Write a problem statement on the basis of your answers to the first question. What is the gap between where you are now and where you want to be? What obstacles prevent easy movement to close the gap?

▶ Write a mission statement, answering the two basic questions:

1. What are we going to do?

2. For whom are we going to do it?

Talk to your customer about these issues. Do not present your written statements to her. Instead, see whether you can get confirmation by asking open-ended questions. If you can't, you may have to revise what you have written.

CHAPTER 5

Creating the Project Risk Plan

A s mentioned in Chapter 1, risk management is the systematic process of identifying, analyzing, and responding to project risk. *Systematic* is a key word here, as many project managers attempt to deal with risks on an informal basis with little or no prior planning. Any project manager who operates in this manner is inviting failure, if not disaster. These are strong words, but appropriate for an important topic. A formal, comprehensive project risk plan allows the project manager to be proactive regarding the innumerable things that can and do go wrong with a project. Without this plan, you are forced to manage reactively when things go wrong—easily the most expensive approach. A systematic process adds discipline and efficiency when creating the plan. At the end of Chapter 4, a high-level overview of the risk process was

> A formal, comprehensive project risk plan allows the project manager to be proactive regarding the innumerable things that can and do go wrong with a project.

presented. Here we present a comprehensive approach to project risk management.

Defining Project Risks

Project risk management begins early in the life cycle. A clear understanding of the risks that face the project must be established. The sources of project risk are almost limitless, emphasizing the need for a well-thought-out, detailed plan. Typical examples include the loss of a key team member, weather emergencies, technical failures, and poor suppliers. This section introduces general concepts of risk and briefly discusses what should be done early in the process.

Many project managers wait too long to assess risk factors and delay the risk plan because they assume they don't know enough yet, that there are too many unknowns. This is a common trap that you should try to avoid. During the initiation phase of the project life cycle, an initial high-level assessment ought to be conducted. You and your team members should take a strategic approach to "what can go wrong" and begin laying the foundation for the detailed plan to follow. Without this foundation, projects often experience the negative impact of risks that become reality, risks that might have been prevented or mitigated through contingency planning. This is *reactive* behavior, and you must live in the *proactive* world to be successful as a project manager. Potential opportunities are sometimes referred to as positive risks, where the project manager strives to optimize the positive impact on project objectives.

As previously noted, project risk management is identified as one of the nine knowledge areas of the *PMBOK® Guide*. The *PMBOK® Guide* describes project

> **Project risk management is "the process of conducting risk management planning, identification, analysis, response planning, and monitoring and control on a project."**

risk management as "*the process of conducting risk management planning, identification, analysis, response planning, and monitoring and control on a project.*" By definition, a process can be considered a formal, controlled undertaking with little or no variation. When applied to processes, variation often equals inefficiency. It is important for you to manage risks formally by applying an agreed-upon process to establish the risk management plan. Given the realities and variables of the typical project environment, a certain amount of flexibility is appropriate. As you gain experience in managing risks, an intuitive feel for flexibility will develop depending upon style and the length, width, depth, and breadth of the projects.

The Six-Step Process

The Six-Step process is a common and practical approach to establishing the project risk plan. This process should not be created in a vacuum but typically involves a great deal of research and collaboration with the project team.

Step 1: Make a List

Brainstorm. Making a list of potential risks to the project should not be an analysis but a formal brainstorming session, when all ideas are captured. Steps 2 and 3 of the process allow for a vetting of these ideas. **| Step 1: Make a list.** It is important that the entire team get involved in identifying threats and highlighting what can go wrong. Some project managers make the mistake of trying to accomplish this on their own to allow team members to complete other tasks. This is shortsighted and a bad idea. This initial step of the process must be collaborative and involve the individuals who are expert at that portion of the project work for which they are responsible. Leverage the intellectual capital (smarts) that is your team. If one or more members are left out, it is likely that some risks will remain unidentified and pose a threat to project success. Remember, involve everyone—a procurement specialist will not be helpful in identifying potential software development problems, and vice versa.

When you work with the support of an informal team, you will need to be disciplined and realize that a certain amount of research is necessary before moving forward. This may include phone calls, e-mails, office visits, or videoconferencing—whatever it takes to elicit the information you need. You typically start with the informal team members or contributors to the project and initiate a dialogue as to what might go wrong. Usually, these discussions identify other ancillary individuals who should be contacted. Functional department managers can be very helpful in these circumstances, either assisting directly or identifying others in their department who can.

In either case, you should take a holistic approach to establishing the list, as all types of risks will need to be identified and dealt with accordingly.

Steps 2 & 3: Determine the Probability of Risk Occurrence and Negative Impact

I am combining steps 2 and 3 because they are the prioritization factors. They assist you in vetting the list of risks. These two steps allow you to prioritize all identified threats to the project and help you determine how much time, effort, staff, and money should be devoted to preventing or mitigating each. Again, this must be accomplished not in a vacuum but with full input from team members and subject matter experts (SMEs).

> **Steps 2 & 3: Determine the probability of risk occurrence and negative impact.**

How probable is it that each risk will become a reality? This question needs to be asked and answered. It is often sufficient to use a High-Medium-Low (HML) scale and apply it to the list of brainstormed risks. If a risk is considered highly probable, it receives an H; if the probability is medium, it receives an M; and if the probability is low, it receives an L. These labels should not be applied arbitrarily, emphasizing the need for team collaboration or research and analysis by the project manager.

If the risk becomes a reality, how badly will it damage the project? This is the next question that needs to be asked and answered. All aspects of the project should be considered when rating the negative impact of any risk. If the risk becomes reality, how will it affect the budget, schedule, resource utilization, scope of work, and so on? The output of steps 2 and 3 results in a list of potential risks with corresponding values for probability and negative impact:

Risk	Probability	Impact
A	M	L
B	M	M
C	L	L
D	H	H

Given the assessment of risks A through D in the table, it is clear that you should focus most of your efforts mitigating risk D and that very little attention should be paid to risk C. Please remember that you could be wrong (unfortunately, I needed to be reminded of this as a young project manager). Just because you label a risk Low probability and Low impact does not guarantee that it will be, so leave it on your radar screen.

For those who prefer metrics, a simple number-based scale can be applied. As you rate probability and impact, you assign a value to each risk. The probability scale can be based on a range of 1 through 10, with 1 representing unlikely and 10 being very likely. Negative impact can be represented by the same scale or in budgetary impact:

Risk	Probability		$ Impact		Total
A	3	×	1K	=	3K
B	7	×	1K	=	7K
C	2	×	14K	=	28K
D	5	×	3K	=	15K

According to this analysis, risk C will demand most of this project team's attention because of its relative value of 28K. It should be noted that the same method can be used to focus on schedule impact or even resource utilization.

Step 4: Prevent or Mitigate the Risk

Some risks can be prevented; others can only be mitigated. Earthquakes or the retirement of an important stakeholder, for instance, cannot be prevented. Some risks can and should be prevented in step 4. If a risk has been identified and you have the ability to prevent its occurrence, do so. Proactivity is the project manager's best friend. Kill the risk before it has a chance to grow and flourish, and you won't have to deal with it again.

Step 4: Prevent or mitigate the risk.

For example, if a vendor or supplier is targeted for your project and one of your team members has had previous dealings with the company and was not impressed, he will inform you that the supplier's material deliveries are frequently late and often rejected. Assuming that the supplier is not a sole source (your only choice), you can prevent the risk by finding an alternate supplier that is more reliable.

For those risks that cannot be prevented, an attempt should be made to mitigate or lessen the probability and/or impact should they occur. Using the example of the unreliable supplier, if you must use that company, you can create concrete steps to proactively expedite the delivery of the material, thereby mitigating the impact of the risk. If management threatens to deprioritize your project, you can lobby on your project's behalf, mitigating the chances that this will occur.

Step 5: Consider Contingencies

Preventive measures are those steps taken before the risk becomes reality. *Contingencies* represent the specific

Step 5: Consider contingencies.

actions that will be taken if the risk occurs. Here, you answer the question "If the risk becomes reality, what will we do"?

For example, if acceptance testing for a supplier's widgets has been identified as medium to high risk and a test failure occurs, an appropriate contingency might be to supply engineering support at the vendor's expense. Another contingency might be to switch to another predetermined vendor if he has widgets in stock.

Contingencies are directly linked to the prioritization factors introduced in steps 2 and 3. If the risk is a high priority (high probability, high negative impact) you will want to identify multiple contingencies. Since there is a good chance that the risk will occur and that when it does, it will hurt the project, you want to be covered. If the risk falls in the middle range of the prioritization scale, you should establish at least one contingency. Those risks that fall in the lower level should not require much attention; it is best to invest your efforts elsewhere. When establishing your contingencies, be careful of the very low probability, very high impact risk. These tend to be totally ignored because of the low probability, but they can and sometimes do bring projects down.

Step 6: Establish the Trigger Point

The trigger point is often the most important element of the project risk plan. There is a direct relationship between the trigger point and the contingencies. True to its name, the *trigger point* is the point at which the risk becomes enough of a reality that the project manager needs to trigger the contingency. It is a judgment call meant to maximize the value of the predetermined contingency by implementing it at the optimal time. Trigger too soon and you will probably spend time, effort, or money for no good reason. Trigger too late and you may end up experiencing the full impact of the occurrence, with little value added by implementing the contingency. Let's return to our example.

> **Step 6: Establish the trigger point.**

If a usually reliable supplier has experienced labor issues and has shut down because of a strike, perhaps your contingency plan has identified suppliers B and C as alternatives. Each has widgets in stock and has quoted a lead time of two calendar weeks for prep and delivery. If the required delivery date is February 15, your trigger should include the two-week lead time plus a few days' buffer. An appropriate trigger point here would be January 31. If the contingency affects a task or tasks on the *critical path* (see Chapter 7), additional buffer days should be considered.

The trigger should be a specific point in time or a defined range of time. Most project managers consider this to be the trickiest part of the project risk plan, but it is well worth the effort. Often, in my role as consultant, I come across well-thought-out plans that were wasted due to untimely or nonexistent contingency implementation. The trigger point is a best practice for project managers that will improve the efficacy of the entire plan.

Establishing Reserves

The most comprehensive risk plan can be compromised if you realize that you do not have the time or means to take appropriate action. Establishing reserves enables you to leverage the plan to its fullest potential. The best-laid plans are impotent without the time and/or budget to allow for effective implementation. As a result, you need to establish contingency and management reserves.

> **The most comprehensive risk plan can be compromised if you realize that you do not have the time or means to take appropriate action.**

Contingency reserves are designated amounts of time and/or budget to account for risks to the project that have been identified and actively accepted. They are created to cover *known* risks to the project. There is a direct relationship between contingency reserves and the previously discussed Six-Step process (or a similar approach). Once the process is complete, you should estimate the required reserves to cover the risks that have been identified and accepted.

For example, if your project team has identified the loss of a key team member to retirement as a high-priority risk (probability and impact), contingency actions will require the hiring of a replacement from outside the organization. The cost and schedule impact of the hiring process and team member assimilation must be estimated and added to the contingency reserve.

Management reserves are designated amounts of time and/or budget included in your plan to account for risks to the project that cannot be predicted. Sometimes you don't know what you don't know. Management reserves are created to cover *unknown* risks to the project. For example, if the current project involves a high percentage of research and development and an analysis of past similar projects using actuals (historical data) indicates an average budgetary overrun of 10 percent, this 10 percent is not attributed to any particular risk event. However, it should trigger the need for a 10 percent increase to the overall project budget as a management reserve.

Managing Multiproject Risks

Many, if not most, project managers find themselves leading more than one project. The multiproject manager confronts unique issues not normally encountered when managing a single project. In the multiproject world, many projects overlap or experience direct dependencies with other projects, similar to those in a typical network diagram (see Chapters 7 and 8).

Two perspectives are required here. First, you must focus on the individual project and the associated risks for each. Then, you must assess your entire portfolio and determine the nature of the relationship of these projects. Your *portfolio* is the sum of all projects under your purview. The relationship among these projects may vary widely.

A *program* typically involves multiple projects working toward the completion of a single deliverable. These projects must all be properly integrated toward this end. In the portfolio environment, you must identify where the projects coincide or overlap with regard to any project work. You then determine what might go wrong in these areas where the projects "touch."

The same is done in the program environment, where project relationships are usually more clearly defined. For example, track and field includes events involving four runners that must pass a baton from one to the other. The fastest team does not always win because the baton may not be handed off smoothly, or it may even be dropped. Many projects will have direct predecessor-successor relationships (one must be completed before the next can begin) in the program world. In order to promote a smooth transition from one project to the next, you must focus on this "baton" handoff. The multiproject risk plan focuses on just these events.

> **A *program* typically involves multiple projects working toward the completion of a single deliverable.**

Coordination Points

In either case, the areas where the projects touch are called *coordination points*. You need to identify these points, after which a standard multiproject risk plan can be created. It is important to emphasize that the Six-Step focus here must be on the coordination points exclusively. In reality, you focus on creating a risk plan for each project individually to manage intraproject risks and then turn your attention to the coordination points and perform the same process to manage interproject risks. The portfolio or program risk plan is meant to supplement and enhance the individual risk plan in the multiproject environment.

Risk Matrix

A useful tool when managing many risks across projects is the standard risk matrix, as shown in Figure 5-1.

Figure 5-1. Risk matrix.

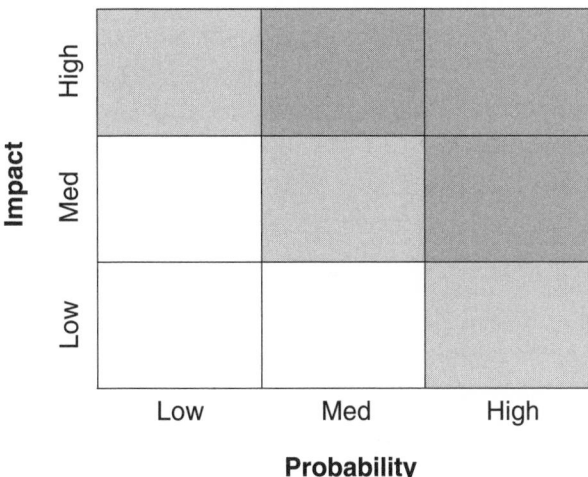

Once the threats have been plotted onto the risk matrix, an H-M-L prioritization can be applied where the highest priority risks are positioned toward the upper right corner and lower priority ones toward the lower left. You can then color code individual risks as they apply to each project. In the fog of the portfolio or program management world, this can prove to be a very effective approach.

Risk Register

The risk register is a useful tool in managing actions taken regarding accepted risks to the project, as shown in Figure 5-2.

Figure 5-2. Risk register.

ID	Risk	Outcome/Response	Owner	P	I	Active

P = Probability   I = Impact

Source: The American Management Association seminar, "Improving Your Project Management Skills: The Basics for Success."

The risk register is the last ingredient of the project risk plan. It is a living, breathing dynamic tool that can help you to track risk status as your project matures through the life cycle. The risk register also helps you identify ownership of contingency implementation, outcomes of actions taken, and active and inactive risks.

If a thorough risk analysis is not developed, you and your team will live in the reactive world, putting out fires throughout the project life cycle. This is easily the most expensive way to operate in terms of time, effort, and money, and it will jeopardize the success of any project. You must invest yourself early by adding this crucial element to your overall project plan.

Key Points to Remember

▶ Project risk management should begin early in the process and continue through the life cycle. A key to success in dealing with risk is to start early and lay the foundation for risk management; be proactive, not reactive; manage risks formally with a *process*; and be flexible.

▶ The Six-Step process to establishing a project risk plan includes making a list of potential risks; determining the probability of risk occurrence; determining its negative impact; preventing or mitigating the risk; considering contingencies; and establishing trigger points for activating contingencies.

▶ Establishing contingency and management reserves enables you to leverage your project risk plan to its fullest potential.

▶ Coordination points must be identified and analyzed in the multiproject risk environment.

▶ A standard risk matrix is a useful tool when managing many risks across projects.

▶ The risk register can be an effective tool for organizing and prioritizing threats to the project.

Exercise . . . .

Choose one of your current or recent projects, and practice the Six-Step process. Make a list of potential risks to the project and prioritize each, utilizing H-M-L or a simple metric-based scale. Pick any three risks and establish:

▶ Prevent measures

▶ Contingencies

▶ Trigger points

Two or three bullet points for each should suffice.

CHAPTER 6

Using the Work Breakdown Structure to Plan a Project

n a previous chapter, I said that planning answers the questions "What must be done?", "How long will it take?", and "How much will it cost?". Planning the *what* is vital; projects frequently fail because a significant part of the work is forgotten. In addition, once tasks have been identified, the time and resource requirements must be determined. This is called *estimating*.

A major problem in project planning is determining how long tasks will take and what it will cost to do them. Inaccurate estimates are a leading cause of project failures, and missed cost targets are a common cause of stress and recrimination in project management.

The most useful tool for accomplishing all of these tasks is the work breakdown structure (WBS). The idea behind the WBS is simple: You can subdivide a complicated task into smaller tasks until you reach a level that cannot be further subdivided. At that point, it is usually easier to estimate how long the small task will take and how much it will cost to perform than it would have been to estimate these factors for the higher levels.

Nevertheless, it is still not easy to estimate task durations for activities that have never been performed before. Because this is the typical situation in engineering hardware and software development projects, we might expect many of these estimates to be in error, and this seems to be demonstrated by experience. Still, the work breakdown structure makes it easier to estimate knowledge tasks than any other tool we have.

A Simple Example

As an example, if I want to clean a room (see Figure 6-1), I might begin by picking up clothes, toys, and other things that have been dropped on the floor. I could use a vacuum cleaner to get dirt out of the carpet. I might wash the windows and wipe down the walls, then dust the furniture. All of these activities are *subtasks* performed to clean the room.

As for vacuuming the room, I might have to get the vacuum cleaner out of the closet, connect the hose, plug it in, push the vacuum cleaner around the room, empty the bag, and put the machine

Figure 6-1. WBS diagram to clean a room.

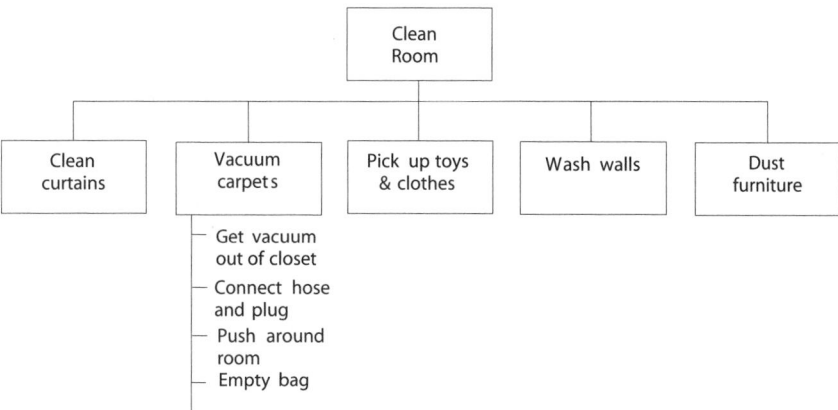

back in the closet. These are still smaller tasks to be performed in accomplishing the subtask called *vacuuming*. The diagram in Figure 6-1 shows how this might be portrayed in WBS format.

Note that we do not worry about the sequence in which work is performed when we do a WBS. That will be worked out when we develop a schedule. However, you will probably find yourself thinking sequentially, as it seems to be human nature to do so. The main idea of doing a WBS is to capture all of the tasks. So if you find yourself and other members of your team thinking sequentially, don't be too concerned, but don't get hung up on trying to diagram the sequence or you will slow down the process of task identification.

> **A work breakdown structure *does not show the sequence in which work is performed!* Such sequencing is determined when a schedule is developed.**

The typical WBS has three to six levels, and these can be named as shown in Figure 6-2. It is, of course, possible to have projects that require a lot more levels. Twenty levels is considered to be the upper limit, and that is a huge project. Note that level 1 is called the *program* level. The difference between a program and a project is just one of degree.

An example of a program is the development of an airplane. For example, the WBS for the program might be drawn as shown in Figure 6-3. Notice that the engine, wing, and avionics are large enough jobs to be called projects in their own right. In fact, the program manager's job is to make sure that the projects are all properly integrated. The engine mounts on the wing, so, somewhere in the structure to develop the engine, there will be an activity called "Design wing mounts." And for the wing, there will be an activity called "Design engine mounts." If these are not coordinated properly, you will wind up with an engine that won't mount on the wing. The job of coordinating these is called *system integration*.

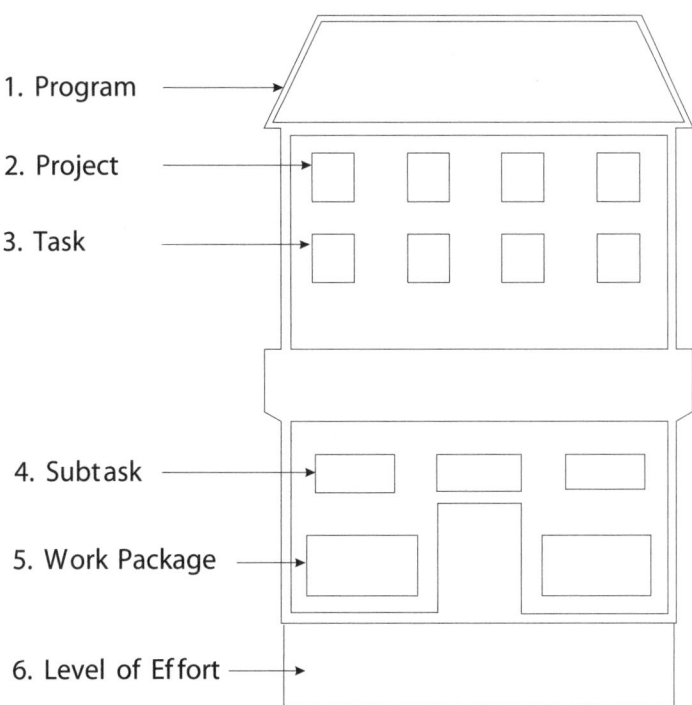

Figure 6-2. WBS level names.

1. Program

2. Project

3. Task

4. Subtask

5. Work Package

6. Level of Effort

Guidelines for Developing the WBS

One important question in constructing a WBS is "When do you stop breaking down the work?" The general guideline is that you stop when you reach a point where either you can estimate time and cost to the desired degree of accuracy or the work will take an amount of time equal to the smallest units you want to schedule. If, for instance, you want to schedule to the nearest day, you break down the work to the point where tasks take about a day to perform. If you are going to schedule to the nearest hour, then you stop when task durations are in that range.

> **Stop breaking down work when you reach a low enough level to do an estimate of the desired accuracy.**

Figure 6-3. Partial WBS.

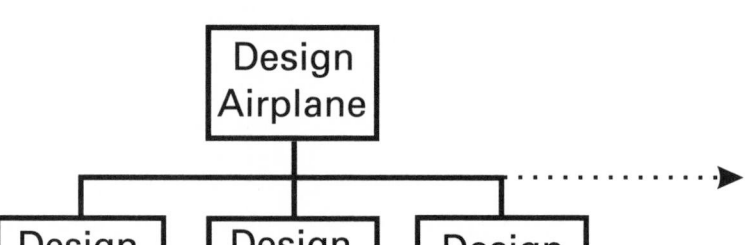

Remember the rule that the people who must do the work should participate in planning it? That applies here. Usually a core group identifies top-level parts of the WBS; those parts are further refined by other members of the team and then integrated to obtain the entire WBS.

One important point: the WBS should be developed before the schedule. In fact, the WBS is the device that ties the entire project together. It allows the manager to assign resources and to estimate time and cost and shows the scope of the job in graphic form. Later, as the project is tracked, the work can be identified as falling in a particular box in the WBS.

There is at least one software package, SuperProject Expert™, that prints a WBS after schedule data have been entered. That is a nice feature, since it

The WBS should always be developed before the schedule is worked out, but without trying to identify the sequence of activities.

gives a graphically attractive WBS, but the rough drawing should be made before you use the scheduling software. The reason is quite simple: Until everyone has agreed that all tasks have been identified, it is misleading to develop a schedule. You cannot be sure that the critical path identified by a partial schedule will be the same for the full schedule.

There are a number of approaches to developing the WBS. Ideally, you proceed top-down, following development of a good problem statement and mission statement. As I have mentioned, however, the mind does not always operate in such nice, linear fashion; as you develop the WBS, you may sometimes find that it helps you to understand the job better. For that reason, I am not a purist about doing things in a specific order. You do what works best for you.

A WBS does not have to be symmetrical. All paths do not have to go down to the same level.

The WBS does not have to be symmetrical. That is, all paths need not be broken down to level 6 (or whatever level you stop at). Since the rule is to break work down to a level sufficient to achieve the estimating accuracy you desire, one path may take six levels, while another may need only three.

Uses of the WBS

As I have said, the WBS is a good way to show the scope of a job. If you have ever given someone an estimate for project cost or time and seen the person's horrified look, you know that the person is seeing the project in her mind as much simpler than it is. When you show a project in WBS form, it is clear to most individuals why the job costs so much.

The WBS is a good way to portray the scope of a project.

In fact, I have had the experience of finding the planning group members themselves overwhelmed by the complexity and magnitude of the WBS. If it impresses them, think of its impact on an outsider.

Assigning responsibility for tasks is another important use of the WBS. Each task to be performed should be assigned to a particular person who will be responsible for its completion. These assignments can then be listed on a separate form, often called a responsibility chart (see Figure 6-4).

Figure 6-4. Responsibility chart.

Linear Responsibility Chart														
Project:			Date Issued:				Sheet Number:		of					
Manager:			Date Revised:				Revision No.		File: LRCFORM.61					
			Project Contributors											
Task Descriptions														

CODES: 1 = ACTUAL RESPONSIBILITY; 2 = SUPPORT; 3 = MUST BE NOTIFIED; BLANK = NOT INVOLVED

Estimating Time, Costs, and Resources

Once the work is broken down, you can estimate how long it will take. But how? Suppose I ask you how long it will take to sort a standard deck of playing cards that has been thoroughly shuffled into numerical order by suit. How would you answer that question?

The most obvious way would be to try the task several times and get a feeling for it. But if you didn't have a deck of cards handy, you would probably think about it, *imagine* how long it would take, and give me an answer. People generally give me answers ranging from two minutes to ten minutes. My tests indicate that about three minutes is average for most adults.

> **An estimate can be made only by starting with the assumption that a certain resource will be assigned.**

Suppose, however, we gave the cards to a child about four or five years old. It might take a lot longer, since the child would not be that familiar with the sequence in which cards are ordered and perhaps not yet even that comfortable with counting. So we must reach a very important conclusion: You cannot do a time or cost estimate without considering who will actually perform the task. Second, you must base the estimate on historical data or a mental model. Historical data are best.

> **Parkinson's Law: Work expands to fill the time allowed.**

Generally, we use average times to plan projects. That is, if it takes three minutes on average for adults to sort a deck of cards, I would use three minutes as my estimate of how long it will take during execution of my project. Naturally, when I use averages, in reality some tasks will take longer than the time allowed, and some should take less. Overall, however, they should *average out.*

That is the idea, anyway. Parkinson's Law discredits this notion, however. Parkinson said that work always expands to fill the time allowed. That means that tasks may take longer than the estimated time, but they almost never take less. One reason is that when people find themselves with some time left, they tend to refine what they have done. Another is that people fear that if they turn work in early, they may be expected to do the task faster the next time or that they may be given more work to do.

> **We must be careful not to penalize workers who perform better than expected by loading them down with excessive work.**

This is a very important point: If people are penalized for performing better than the target, they will quit doing so. We also have to understand *variation.* If the same person sorts a deck of cards over and over, we know the sort times will vary. Sometimes it will take two minutes, while other times it will take four.

> **An exact estimate is an oxymoron!**

The average may be three, but we may expect that half the time it will take three minutes or less and half the time it will take three minutes or more. Very seldom will it take *exactly* three minutes.

The same is true for *all* project tasks. The time it takes to perform them will vary, because of forces outside the person's control. The cards are shuffled differently every time. The person's attention is diverted by a loud noise outside. He drops a card while sorting. He gets tired. And so on.

Can you get rid of the variation? No way.

Can you reduce it? Yes—through practice, by changing the process by which the work is done, and so on. But it is important to note that the variation will always be there, and we must recognize and accept it.

The Hazards of Estimating

Consider the case of Karen. One day, her boss stopped by her desk at about one o'clock. "Need for you to do an estimate for me," he told her. "Promised the Big Guy I'd have it for him by four o'clock. You with me?"

Karen nodded and gave him a thin smile. The boss described the job for her. "Just need a ballpark number," he assured her and drifted off.

Given so little time, Karen could compare the project her boss described only to one she had done about a year before. She added a little for this and took a little off for that, put in some contingency to cover her lack of information, and gave the estimate to the boss. After that, she forgot all about the job.

Two months passed. Then the bomb was dropped. Her boss appeared, all smiles. "Remember that estimate you did for me on the xyz job?"

She had to think hard to remember, but, as her boss droned on, it came back to her. He piled a big stack of specifications on her desk. "It's your job now," he told her and drifted off again into manager dreamland.

As she studied the pile of paper, Karen felt herself growing more concerned. There were significant differences between this set of specs and what her boss had told her when she did the estimate. "Oh, well, I'm sure he knows that," she told herself.

Finally, she managed to work up a new estimate for the job on the basis of the real specs. It was almost 50 percent higher than the ballpark figure. She checked her figures carefully, assured herself that they were correct, and went to see her boss.

He took one look at the numbers and went ballistic. "What are you trying to do to me?" he yelled. "I already told the old man we would do it for the original figure. I can't tell him it's this much more. He'll kill me."

"But you told me it was just a ballpark number you needed," Karen argued. "That's what I gave you. But this is nothing like the job I quoted. It's a lot bigger."

"I can't help that," her boss argued. "I already gave him the figures. You'll have to find a way to do it for the original bid."

Naturally, you know the rest of the story. The job cost even more than Karen's new estimate. There was a lot of moaning and groaning, but, in the end, Karen survived. Oh, they did send her off to a course on project management—hoping, no doubt, that she would learn how to estimate better in the future.

> **One of the primary causes of project failures is that ballpark estimates become targets.**

Here are some guidelines for documenting estimates:

- ▶ Show the percent tolerance that is likely to apply.

- ▶ Tell how the estimate was made and what assumptions were used.

- ▶ Specify any factors that might affect the validity of the estimate (such as whether the estimate will still be valid in six months).

Could you fault Karen for anything? Well, perhaps. If she failed to tell the boss that a ballpark estimate might have a tolerance of perhaps ± 25 percent but that the margin of error could range from -10 percent to $+100$ percent, then she allowed him to think that the estimate was better than it was. Also, she should have documented all working assumptions, explaining how she did the estimate, what project she had used for comparison, and so on. Then, if management still pulled a whammy on her, at least she would have had some protection. In fact, it is impossible to make sense of any estimate unless these steps are taken, so they should be standard practice.

Consensual Estimating

In recent years, a new method of estimating knowledge work has been developed that seems to work better than older techniques. Rather than have individuals estimate task durations, the new method asks at least three people to estimate each activity in the project that they know something about. They do this without discussing their ideas with one another. They then meet to find out what they have put on paper. In a typical situation, there may be a range of times, such as, for example, ten days, twelve days, and thirty days, in which two of the estimates are close together, but one is very different. How do you handle the discrepancy?

The best approach is to discuss what each person was considering when he made the estimate. It may be that the person who put down thirty days was thinking about something that the other two had overlooked. Or, conversely, the other two might convince the thirty-day person that his number is way too high and get him to come down to a figure nearer their estimates. In any case, they try to arrive at a number that they all can support. This is called *consensus*.

There are three advantages to this approach. First, no one person is on the hook for the final number. Second, inexperienced people learn to estimate from those more experienced. Third, several people are likely to collectively consider more issues than any one person would do working alone. For that reason, you are more likely to get an accurate estimate, although it is important to remember that it is still by definition not exact!

Improving Estimating Ability

People cannot learn unless they receive feedback on their performance. If you went out every day and ran one hundred yards, trying to improve your speed, but you never timed yourself, you would have no idea whether you were getting better or worse. You could be doing something that slowed you down, but you wouldn't know it. In the same way, if you estimate task durations but never record the actual time it takes to do the task, you are never going to get better at estimating. Furthermore, you have to track progress by recording times daily. If you record times once a week, I can promise you that you will be just guessing, and that won't be helpful.

Key Points to Remember

▶ Do not try to work out sequencing of activities when you develop a WBS. You will do that when you develop a schedule.

▶ A WBS ties the entire project together. It portrays scope graphically, allows you to assign resources, permits you to develop estimates of time and costs, and thus provides the basis for the schedule and the budget.

▶ An estimate is a *guess*, and an exact estimate is an *oxymoron*!

▶ Be careful that ballpark estimates don't become targets.

▶ Consensual estimating is a good way to deal with activities for which no history exists.

▶ No learning takes place without feedback. Estimate; then track your actual time if you want to improve your estimating ability.

Exercise . . . .

Following is a list of tasks to be performed in preparation for a camping trip. Draw a WBS that places the tasks in their proper relationship to one another. The solution is contained in the Answers section.

▶ Arrange for supplies and equipment.

▶ Select campsite.

▶ Make site preparations.

▶ Make site reservation.

▶ Arrange time off from work.

▶ Select route to site.

▶ Prepare menu for meals.

▶ Identify source of supplies and equipment.

▶ Load car.

▶ Pack suitcases.

▶ Purchase supplies.

▶ Arrange camping trip (project).

CHAPTER 7

Scheduling Project Work

One of the primary features that distinguishes project management from general management is the special attention to scheduling. Remember from Chapter 1 that Dr. J. M. Juran says a project is a problem scheduled for solution.

Unfortunately, some people think that project management is nothing but scheduling, and this is incorrect. Scheduling is just one of the tools used to manage jobs and should not be considered the primary one.

Project management is not just scheduling.

People today tend to acquire scheduling software, of which there is an abundance, and think that will make them instant project managers. They soon find that that idea is wrong. In fact, it is nearly impossible to use the software effectively unless you understand project management (and scheduling methodology in particular).

I do have one suggestion about soft-

Suggestion: Whatever scheduling software you choose, get some professional training on how to use it.

ware. Whatever you pick, get some professional training on how to use it. In the early days of personal computers, there was a pretty significant difference between the low-end and the high-end software that was available. The low-end packages were pretty easy to use, whereas the high-end ones were not. The gap between low- and high-end software has closed to the point that this is no longer true. They are *all* difficult to use now, and the training materials (tutorials and manuals) that come with the software are often not very good. In addition, it is hard to find time to work through a tutorial without being interrupted several times, which means that self-learning is difficult. The most efficient way is to take a class.

Do check out the instructor's knowledge of project management before choosing which class to take. Some of the people teaching the software know very little about project management itself, and, when you have questions, they can't answer them.

You should expect to spend from two to three days of classroom time becoming really proficient with the software. That is still a good investment, considering the time the software can save you in the long run.

A Brief History of Scheduling

Until around 1958, the only tool for scheduling projects was the bar chart (see Figure 7-1). Because Henry Gantt developed a complete notational system for showing progress with bar charts, they are often called Gantt charts. They are simple to construct and read and remain the best tool to use for communicating to team members what they need to do within given time frames. Arrow diagrams tend to be too complicated for some teams. Nevertheless, it is often helpful to show an arrow diagram to the people doing the work so that they understand interdependencies and why it is important that they complete certain tasks on time.

Bar charts do have one serious drawback—it is very difficult to determine the impact of a slip on one task on the rest of the

Figure 7-1. Bar chart.

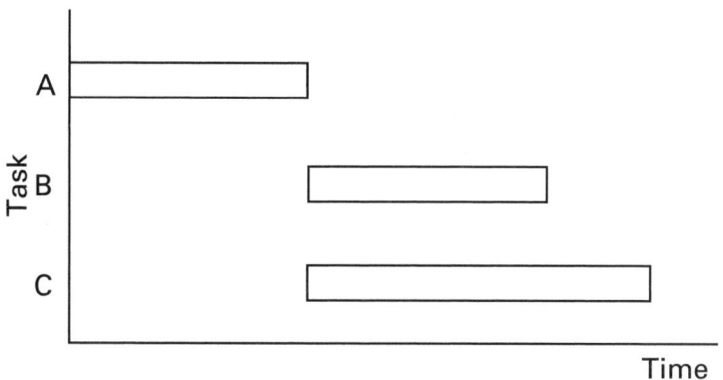

project (e.g., if Task A in Figure 7-1 gets behind, it is hard to tell how this will affect the rest of the work). The reason is that the bar chart (in its original format) did not show the interdependencies of the work. (Contemporary software does show links between bars, making them easier to read. The actual name for these bar charts is "time-line critical path schedules.")

To overcome this problem, two methods of scheduling were developed in the late 1950s and early 1960s, both of which use arrow diagrams to capture the sequential and parallel relationships among project activities. One of these methods, developed by Du Pont, is called *Critical Path Method* (CPM), and the other, developed by the U.S. Navy and the Booz Allen Hamilton consulting group, is called *Program Evaluation and Review Technique* (PERT). Although it has become customary to call all arrow diagrams PERT networks, strictly speaking the PERT method makes use of probability techniques, whereas CPM does not. In other words, with PERT it is possible to calculate the probability that an activity will be completed by a certain time, whereas that is not possible with CPM.

CPM: Critical Path Method

PERT: Program Evaluation and Review Technique

Network Diagrams

To show the sequence in which work is performed, diagrams like those in Figure 7-2 are used. In these diagrams, Task A is done before B, while Task C is done in parallel with them.

The network in the bottom half of Figure 7-2 uses *activity-on-arrow* notation, in which the arrow represents the work being done and the circle represents an event. An event is *binary*; that is, it has either occurred or it has not. An activity, on the other hand, can be partially complete. Note that this is a special use of the word "event." We speak of a football game as an event, even though it spans time. In scheduling terminology, however, an *event* is a specific point in time where something has just started or has just been finished.

Figure 7-2. Arrow diagrams.

An activity-on-node network

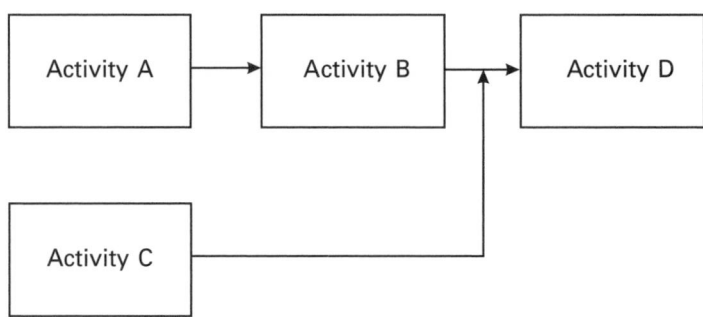

An activity-on-arrow network

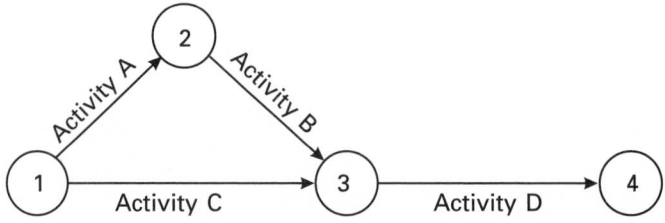

The network in the top half of Figure 7-2 uses *activity-on-node* notation, which shows the work as a box or node, and the arrows show the sequence in which the work is performed. Events are not shown in activity-on-node networks unless they are *milestones*—points in the project at which major portions of the work are completed.

Why two forms of diagrams? Probably a tyranny to confuse the uninitiated. Actually, it simply happens that the schemes were developed by different practitioners.

Is one better than the other? No. They both get the same results in figuring out when work is supposed to be completed. Both forms are still used, although activity-on-node is used a bit more than the other, simply because much of today's personal computer software is programmed to use node notation.

What is the benefit of using either CPM or PERT? The main advantage is that you can tell whether it is possible to meet an important project completion date, and you can also tell exactly when various tasks must be finished in order to meet that deadline. Furthermore, you can tell which tasks have some leeway and which do not. In fact, both CPM and PERT determine the *critical path*, which is defined as the longest series of activities (that can't be done in parallel) and which therefore governs how early the project can be completed.

> **The *critical path* is the longest path through a project network. Because it has no slack, all activities on the critical path must be completed as scheduled, or the end date will begin to slip—one day for each day a critical activity is delayed.**

The Reason for Scheduling

Naturally, the primary reason for scheduling a project is to ensure that the deadline can be met. Most projects have a deadline imposed. Furthermore, since the critical path method helps identify which activities will determine the end date, it also helps guide how the project should be managed.

However, it is easy to get carried away with scheduling and spend all of your time updating, revising, and so on. The scheduling software in use today should be viewed as a *tool*, and managers should not become slaves to the tool.

It is also very easy to create schedules that look good on paper but don't work in practice. The main reason is usually that resources are not available to do the work when it comes due. In fact, unless resource allocation is handled properly, schedules are next to useless. Fortunately, today's scheduling software handles resource allocation fairly well, but we leave discussion of the methods used to the software manuals. In this book, we simply examine how networks are used to show us where we need to manage.

> **One company found that when it stopped having people work on multiple projects, workers' productivity *doubled!***

I am often told that scope and priorities change so often in a given organization that it doesn't make sense to spend time finding critical paths. There are two points worth considering here. One is that if scope is changing often in a project, not enough time is being spent doing upfront definition and planning. Scope changes most often occur because something is forgotten. Better attention to what is being done in the beginning usually reduces scope creep.

Second, if priorities are changing often, management does not have its act together. Generally, the organization is trying to tackle too much work for the number of resources available. We all have "wish lists" of things we want to do personally, but we have to put some of them on hold until time, money, or both become available. The same is true of organizations. Experience shows that when you have individuals working on many projects, productivity suffers. One company found, as an example, that when it stopped having people work on multiple projects, employees' productivity *doubled!* That obviously is highly significant.

What does CPM have to do with this? Knowing where the critical path is in a project allows you to determine the impact on the project of a scope or priority change. You know which activities will be impacted most heavily and what might need to be done to regain lost time. In addition, managers can make informed decisions when you can tell them the impact of changes to the project. Thus, CPM can be an invaluable tool when used properly.

Definitions of Network Terms

ACTIVITY
: An *activity* always consumes time and may also consume resources. Examples include paperwork, labor, negotiations, machinery operations, and lead times for purchased parts or equipment.

CRITICAL
: A *critical activity* or event is one that must be achieved by a certain time, having no latitude (slack or float) whatsoever.

CRITICAL PATH
: The *critical path* is the longest path through a network and determines the earliest completion of project work.

EVENTS
: Beginning and ending points of activities are known as *events*. An event is a specific point in time. Events are commonly denoted graphically by a circle and may carry identity nomenclature (e.g., words, numbers, alphanumeric codes).

MILESTONE
: *Milestones* are events that represent a point in a project of special significance. Usually, it is the completion of a major phase of the work. Project reviews are often conducted at milestones.

NETWORK
: Networks are called "arrow diagrams." They provide a graphical representation of a project plan showing the relationships of the activities.

Constructing an Arrow Diagram

As was pointed out in Chapter 6, a work breakdown structure (WBS) should be developed before work on the project is scheduled. Also, we saw that a WBS can contain from two to twenty levels. To illustrate how a schedule is constructed from a WBS, we consider a simple job of maintaining the yard around a home. The WBS is shown in Figure 7-3.

In the case of this WBS, it is appropriate to schedule the tasks at the lowest level. However, this is not always true. Sometimes work is broken down to level 6 but only activities up to level 5 are entered into the schedule. The reason is that you may not be able to keep level 6 tasks on schedule. That is, you can't manage that tightly. So you schedule at a level that you can **Don't schedule in more detail than you can manage.** manage. This follows the general rule that you should never plan (or schedule) in more detail than you *can* manage. Some projects, such as overhauling a large power generator, are scheduled

Figure 7-3. WBS to do yard project.

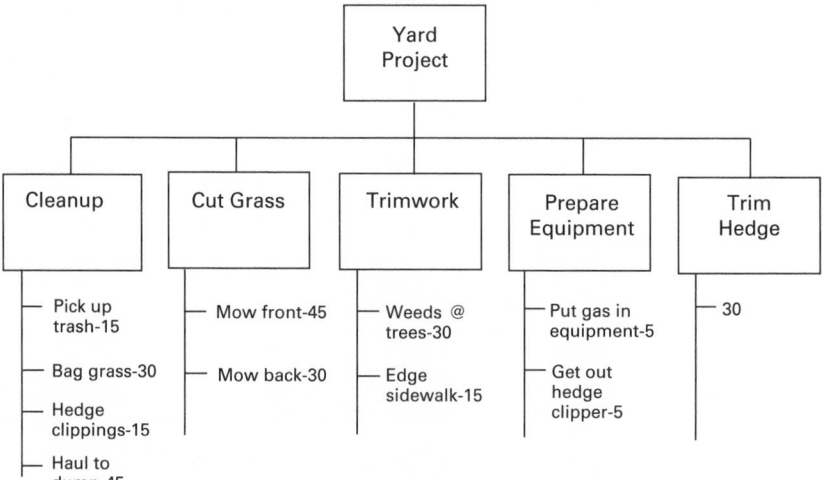

in increments of hours. Others are scheduled in days, while some big construction jobs are scheduled to the nearest month.

While planning in too much detail is undesirable, if you plan in too little detail, you might as well not bother. As a practical example, a manager told me that his staff wanted to create schedules showing tasks with twenty-six-week durations. He protested that the staff would never complete such schedules on time. They would *back-end load* them, he argued.

What he meant was that there is a lot of security in a twenty-six-week task. When the start date comes, if the person doing the task is busy, she might say, "I can always make up a day on a twenty-six-week activity. I'll get started tomorrow." This continues until she realizes she has delayed too long. Then there is a big flurry of activity as she tries to finish on time. All the work has been pushed out to the end of the twenty-six-week time frame.

A good rule of thumb to follow is that no task should have a duration much greater than four to six weeks. A twenty-six-week task can probably be broken down into five or six subtasks. Such a plan generally keeps people from back-end loading.

> A *good* rule of thumb to follow is that no task should have a duration much greater than four to six weeks. For knowledge work, durations should be in the range of one to three weeks, because knowledge work is harder to track than tangible work.

There are two ways you can develop a schedule. One is to begin at the end and work back until you arrive at the beginning. The second method is to start at the beginning and work toward the end. Usually, it is easiest to start at the beginning.

The first step is to decide what can be done first. Sometimes, several tasks can start at the same time. In that case, you simply draw them side by side and start working from there. Note the

Figure 7-4. CPM diagram for yard project.

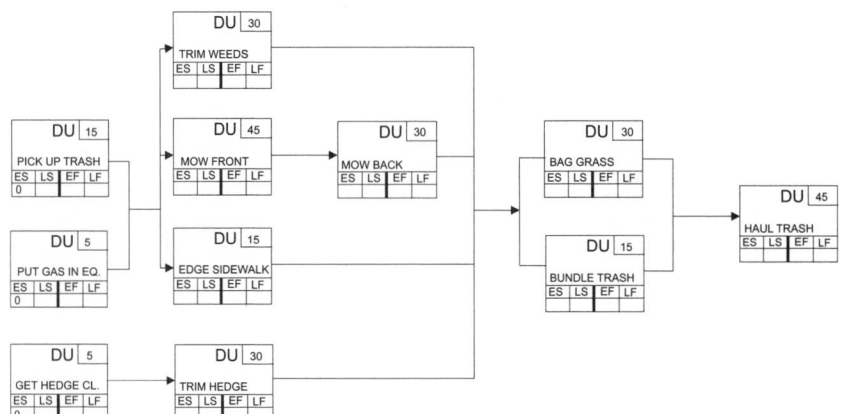

progression in the diagram in Figure 7-4. It sometimes takes several iterations before the sequencing can be worked out completely.

This small project might be thought of as having three phases: *preparation, execution,* and *cleanup.* There are three preparation tasks: *pick up trash, put gas in equipment,* and *get out hedge clipper.* The cleanup tasks include *bagging grass, bundling clippings,* and *hauling trash* to the dump.

In doing this schedule diagram, I have followed a rule of scheduling, which is to *diagram what is logically possible, then deal with resource limitations.* For a yard project, if I have no one helping me, then there really can be no parallel paths. On the other hand, if I can enlist help from the family or neighborhood youth, then parallel paths are possible, so this rule says

Schedules should be developed according to what is logically possible, and resource allocation should be done later. This will yield the optimum schedule.

go ahead and schedule *as if* it were possible to get help. This is especially important to remember in a work setting, or you will never get a schedule put together. You will be worrying about who will be available to do the work and end up in analysis paralysis.

Another rule is to keep all times in the same increments. Don't mix hours and minutes—schedule everything in minutes, then convert to hours and minutes as a last step. For this schedule, I have simply kept everything in minutes.

I suggest that you draw your network on paper and check it for logical consistency before entering anything into a computer scheduling program. If the network has logical errors, the computer will just give you a *garbage-in, garbage-out* result, but it will look impressive, having come from a computer.

Another rule is to keep all times in the same increments.

It is also important to remember that there is usually no *single* solution to a network problem. That is, someone else might draw the arrow diagram a bit differently than you have done. There may be parts of the diagram that *have* to be done in a certain order, but often there is flexibility. For example, you can't deliver papers until you have printed them, so if the diagram showed that sequence, it would be wrong. The conclusion is that there is no single right solution, but a diagram can be said to be wrong if it violates logic.

The network for the yard project could get a lot more complicated. You could have *edge front sidewalk* and *edge back sidewalk*. You could talk about trimming around trees in both front and back, and so on. But there is no need to make it too complicated. We don't usually try to capture *exactly* how we will do the work, just the gist of it.

It is hard to tell whether a network is absolutely correct, but it can be said to be wrong if logic is violated.

The next step is to figure out how long it will take to do the job. Time estimates for each task are made by using history, taking into account how long each activity has taken in the past. Remember, though, that the estimate is valid only for the individual who is going to do the task. If my daughter, who is sixteen, does the lawn mowing using a push mower, it will probably take less time than if my son, who is only twelve, does the same task. In the following chapter, we see how to find the critical path through the network so that we can know how long it will take.

Key Points to Remember

▶ Project management is not just scheduling.

▶ Arrow diagrams allow an easier assessment of the impact of a slip on a project than is possible with Gantt charts.

▶ Schedule at a level of detail that can be managed.

▶ No task should be scheduled with a duration much greater than four to six weeks. Subdivide longer tasks to achieve this objective. Software and engineering tasks should be divided even further, to durations not exceeding one to three weeks.

Exercise

For the following WBS **(Figure 7-5)**, draw an arrow diagram. One solution is shown in the Answers section.

Figure 7-5. WBS to clean room.

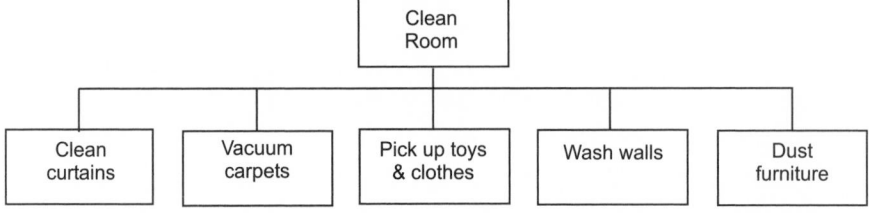

CHAPTER 8

Producing a Workable Schedule

Once a suitable network has been drawn, with durations assigned to all activities, it is necessary to determine where the longest path is in the network and to see whether it will meet the target completion date. Since the longest path through the project determines *minimum* project duration, any activity on that path that takes longer than planned will cause the end date to slip accordingly, so that path is called the *critical path*.

Schedule Computations

Normally, you would let a computer do these computations for you, so you may wonder why it is necessary to know how to do them manually. My belief is that unless you know how the computations are done, you do not fully understand the meanings of float, early and late dates, and so on. Further, you can easily fall prey to the *garbage-in, garbage-out* malady. So here is a brief treatment of how the calculations are done by the computer. (For most schedules, the computer has the added bonus of converting times to calendar dates, which is no easy task to do manually.)

First, consider what we want to know about the project. If it starts at some *time = zero*, we want to know how soon it can be finished. Naturally, in most actual work projects, we have been told when we must be finished. That is, the end date is dictated. Furthermore, the start date for the job is often constrained for some reason: resources won't be available, specs won't be written, or another project won't be finished until that time. So scheduling usually means trying to fit the work between two fixed points in time. Whatever the case, we still want to know how long the project will take to complete; if it won't fit into the required time frame, then we will have to do something to shorten the critical path.

> **Failure to consider resource allocation in scheduling almost always leads to a schedule that cannot be achieved.**

In the simplest form, network computations are made for the network on the assumption that activity durations are exactly as specified. However, activity durations are a function of the level of resources applied to the work, and, if that level is not actually available when it comes time to do the work, then the scheduled dates for the task cannot be met. It is for this reason that network computations must ultimately be made with resource limitations in mind. Another way to say this is that *resource allocation* is necessary to determine what kind of schedule is actually *achievable!* Failure to consider resources almost always leads to a schedule that cannot be met.

> **Initial schedule computations are made assuming that unlimited resources are available. This yields the best-case solution.**

Still, the first step in network computations is to determine where the critical path is in the schedule and what kind of latitude is available for noncritical work, under *ideal conditions*. Naturally, the ideal situation is one in which unlimited resources are available, so the first computations made for the network are done without consideration of resource requirements. It is this method that is described in this chapter, and resource allocation methods are deferred to scheduling software manuals, as I said previously.

Network Rules

In order to compute network start and finish times, only two rules apply to all networks. These are listed as rules 1 and 2. Other rules are sometimes applied by the scheduling software itself. These are strictly a function of the software and are not applied to *all* networks.

Rule 1.   Before a task can begin, all tasks preceding it must be completed.

Rule 2.   Arrows denote the logical order of work.

Basic Scheduling Computations

Scheduling computations are illustrated using the network in Figure 8-1. First, let us examine the node boxes in the schedule. Each has the notations ES, LS, EF, LF, and DU. These mean:

ES = Early Start

LS = Late Start

EF = Early Finish

LF = Late Finish

DU = Duration (of the task)

Forward-Pass Computations

Consider a single activity in the network, such as picking up trash from the yard. It has a duration of fifteen minutes. Assuming that it starts at *time = zero*, it can finish as early as fifteen minutes later. Thus, we can enter 15 in the cell labeled EF.

Figure 8-1. Network to illustrate computation methods.

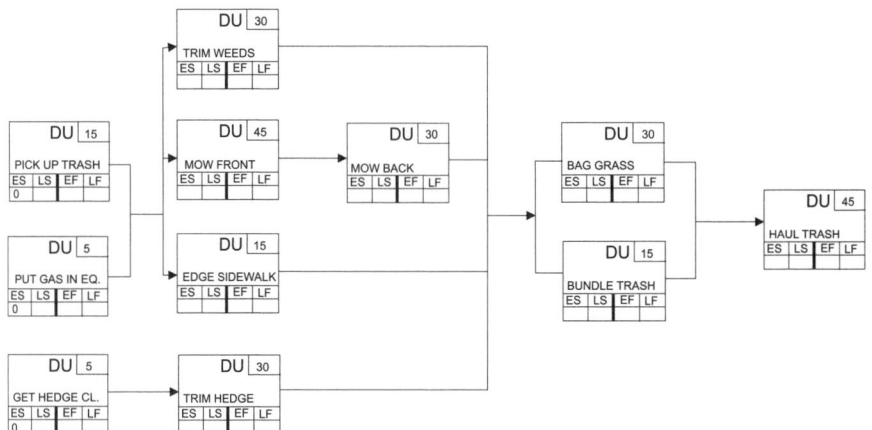

Putting gas in the mower and the weed whacker takes only five minutes. The logic of the diagram says that both of these tasks must be completed before we can begin trimming weeds,

cutting the front grass, and edging the sidewalk. The cleanup task takes fifteen minutes, whereas the gas activity takes only five minutes. How soon can the following activities start? Not until the cleanup has been finished, since it is the longest of the preceding activities.

In fact, then, the Early Finish for cleanup becomes the Early Start for the next three tasks. It is always true that the *latest Early Finish* for preceding tasks becomes the *Early Start* for subsequent tasks. That is, the longest path determines how early subsequent tasks can start.

Following this rule, we can fill in Earliest Start times for each task, as shown in Figure 8-2. This shows that the project will take a total of 165 minutes to complete, if all work is conducted exactly as shown. We have just performed what

> **The Earliest Start for a task is the *latest* Late Finish of preceding tasks. That is, the longest path determines the earliest that a following task can be started.**

Figure 8-2. Diagram with EF times filled in.

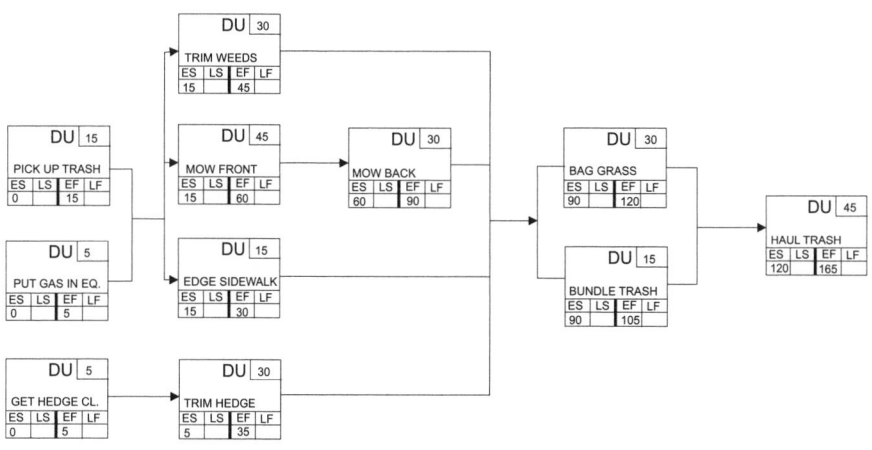

are called *forward-pass computations* to determine Earliest Finish times for all activities. Computer programs do exactly the same thing and additionally convert the times to calendar dates, making quick work of the computations.

> RULE: When two or more activities precede another activity, the earliest time when that activity can be started is the *longer* of the durations of the activities preceding it.

> NOTE: The time determined for the end or final event is the earliest finish for the project in working time. Once weekends, holidays, and other breaks in the schedule are accounted for, the end *date* may be considerably later than the earliest finish in working time.

Backward-Pass Computations

A backward pass is made through the network to compute the *latest start and latest finish times* for each activity in the network. To do that, we must decide how late the project can finish. By convention, we generally don't want a project to end any later than its earliest possible completion. To stretch it out longer would be inefficient.

We also won't insist (for now) that the project end earlier than the earliest possible finish calculated in the previous steps. If we want to finish earlier, we will have to redraw the network or shorten some activities (e.g., by applying more resources or working more efficiently). For now, we will accept the 165-minute working time and let it be the *Latest Finish* for the project.

When doing backward-pass calculations, always use the smallest number for the LF of previous activities.

If Hauling Away Trash has a Late Finish of 165 minutes and has a duration of 45 minutes, what is the latest that it could start? Clearly, if we subtract 45 from 165, we have 120 minutes, which is the Latest Start for the task. Proceeding in this manner, we get LS times for Bagging Grass and Bundling Clippings of 90 and 105 minutes, respectively. One of these two numbers must be the LF time for each of the preceding activities. Which one?

Well, assume we try 105 minutes. If we do that, the schedule would say that Bagging Grass could start as late as 105 minutes, since subsequent tasks can begin as soon as preceding tasks are finished. But if we add 30 minutes for Bagging to the 105-minute ES time, we will finish at 135 minutes, which is later than the 120 minutes previously determined, and we will miss the 165-minute end time for the project.

When an activity has no float, it is called *critical*, since failure to complete work as scheduled will cause the end date to slip.

Therefore, when we are doing *backward-pass calculations*, the *Latest Finish* for a preceding task will always be the *smallest* of the *Late Start* times for the subsequent tasks. (A simpler way to say this is: Always use the smallest number!)

RULE: When two or more activities follow another, the latest time that the preceding activity can be achieved is the *smaller* of the times.

Now examine the path in Figure 8-3 that includes activities highlighted by bold lines. Each activity has the same ES/LS and EF/LF times. There is no *float* (or latitude for slippage) on this path. By convention, an activity with no float is called *critical*, and a total path with no float is called the *critical path*, which means that if any of the work on this path falls behind schedule, then the end date will slip accordingly. All of the activities that have ES/LS or EF/LF times that differ are said to have float. For example, Trim Weeds has an ES time of fifteen minutes and an LS time of sixty minutes, giving it forty-five minutes of float.

The final network is shown in Figure 8-3. Note that some tasks have the same EF and LF times, as well as the same ES and LS times. These tasks are on the *critical path*. In Figure 8-3, they are shown with bold outlines, to indicate exactly where the critical path lies.

The critical path activities have no latitude. They must be completed as scheduled or the entire project will take longer than 165 minutes. Knowing where the critical path is tells a manager where his attention must be applied. The other tasks have latitude, or float. This does not mean that they can be ignored, but they have less chance of delaying the project if they encounter problems. The Edge Sidewalk task, for example, has an ES time of fifteen minutes and an LS time of seventy-five. The difference between the two is sixty minutes, which is the float for the task.

What good is the float? Well, we know we can start the task as late as seventy-five minutes into the job and still finish the project on time. If your son is doing this task, he can watch a sixty-minute television program during that time and still get his Edging task done on time.

Remember, too, that the times are all *estimates*. This means that tasks might take more or less than the scheduled time. So long as they do not take longer than the scheduled time plus the available float time, the job can be completed on time. Critical tasks, which have no float, must be managed in such a way that they take the scheduled time. This is usually done by adjusting the resources (effort) applied, either by assigning more resources or by working overtime (increasing resources in either case).

Figure 8-3. Diagram showing critical path.

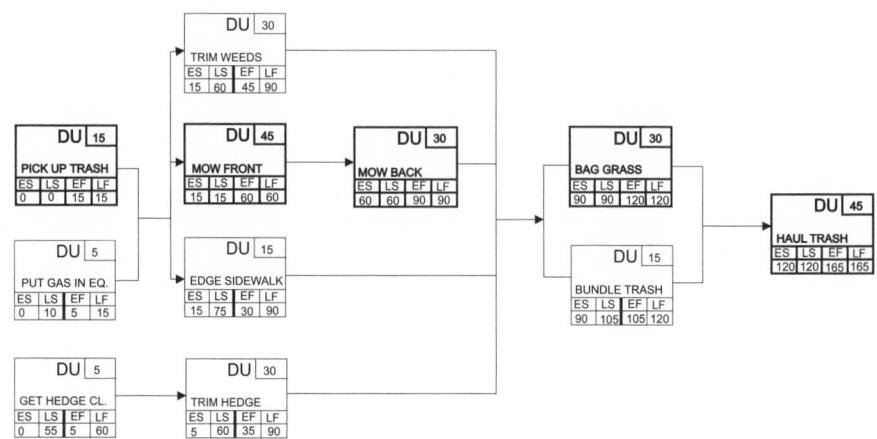

This is not always possible. Applying overtime often increases errors, leading to rework, which may mean that you don't get the job done any faster than if you had just worked a normal schedule. Furthermore, there is always a point of diminishing returns when you add *bodies* to a task. At some point, they just get in each other's way, actually slowing work down rather than speeding it. Note that overtime should be kept in reserve in case of problems, so it is never a good idea to schedule a project in a way that requires overtime just to meet the original schedule.

Another point of great importance: All members of the project team should be encouraged to keep float times in reserve as insurance against bad estimates or unforeseen problems. People tend to wait until the latest possible start time to start a task; then, when problems occur, they miss the end date. If there is no float left, when the task takes longer than originally planned,

> It is bad practice to schedule a project so that overtime is required to meet the schedule, since if problems are encountered, it may not be possible to work more overtime to solve them.

it will impact the end date for the entire project, since, *once a task runs out of float*, it becomes part of the critical path! In fact, the true meaning of the word "critical" is that there is no float. The task must be done on time.

Using the Network to Manage the Project

As I have indicated previously, the point of developing a CPM diagram is to use it to *manage* the project. If this is not done, scheduling is simply a worthless exercise. So here are some pointers that I have found helpful in managing my own jobs:

> **Once you have used up the float on a task, it becomes part of the critical path.**

▶ Try to *stay on schedule.* It is always harder to catch up than to stay on target to begin with.

▶ Keep float in reserve in case of unexpected problems or bad estimates.

▶ Apply whatever effort is needed to keep critical tasks on schedule. If a task on the critical path can be finished ahead of schedule, *do it!* Then start the next task.

▶ Avoid the temptation to perfect everything—that's what the next-generation product or service is all about. Note: I *did not say* it is okay to do the job sloppily or that you shouldn't do your best work. I said don't be tempted to make it *perfect.* By definition, you will never reach perfection.

▶ Estimates of task durations are made on the assumption that certain people will work on those tasks. If someone else is actually used, you may have to adjust durations accordingly. This is especially true if the new person is less skilled than the intended resource.

▶ This was stated in Chapter 7 but is repeated here because of its importance: No task should be scheduled with a duration much greater than four to six weeks. If you do, people tend to have a false sense of security and put off starting, under the assumption "I can always make up one day." By the time they start, they often have slipped several days and find that they cannot finish as scheduled. We say that they *back-end load* the task by pushing all the effort toward the back end. If a task has a duration greater than six weeks, it is a good idea to subdivide it, creating an artificial break if necessary. Then review progress at that point. That will help keep it on target.

▶ If the people doing the work did not develop the network, explain it to them and show them the meaning of float. Don't hide it from them. However, give them a bar chart to work to—it is much easier to read a bar chart than a network diagram. Show them that if they use up float on a given task, then the following tasks may become critical, leaving the people who must do those activities feeling really stressed.

▶ It is possible to shorten a task by adding resources, reducing its scope, doing sloppy (poor-quality) work, being more efficient, or changing the process by which the work is done. With the exception of doing sloppy work, all of the methods may be acceptable. A reduction in scope must be negotiated with your customer, of course.

▶ Scheduling is done initially on the assumption that you will have the resources you planned on having. If people are shared with other projects or if you plan to use the same person on several tasks, you may find that you have her overloaded. Modern software generally warns you that you have overloaded your resources and may be able to help you solve the problem.

Converting Arrow Diagrams to Bar Charts

While an arrow diagram is essential to do a proper analysis of the relationships between the activities in a project, the best working tool is the bar chart. The people doing the work will find it much easier to see when they are supposed to start and finish their jobs if you give them a bar chart. The arrow diagram in Figure 8-3 has been portrayed as a bar chart in Figure 8-4, making use of what was learned about the schedule from the network analysis.

Figure 8-4. Bar chart schedule for yard project.

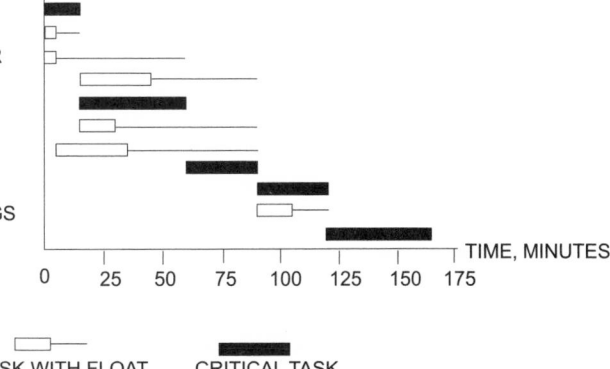

Note that the critical path in the bar chart is shown as solid black bars. Bars with float are drawn hollow with a line trailing to indicate how much float is available. The task can end as late as the point at which the trailing line ends.

This is fairly conventional notation. Scheduling software always allows you to print a bar chart, even though a CPM network is used to find the critical path and to calculate floats. One caution: Many programs display the critical path in red on a color monitor and often color started tasks with green or blue. When these bars are printed on a black-and-white printer, all of them may look black, implying that they are all critical, confusing the people trying to read them. It is usually possible to have the computer display shading or cross-hatching instead of color so that when they are printed in black-and-white, there will be no ambiguity.

Assigning Resources to Tasks

I have already said that the first step in developing a schedule is to assume that you have unlimited resources, because this is the best situation you can ever assume, and if you can't meet your project completion date with an unlimited resource schedule, you may as well know it early. However, once you have determined that the end date can somehow be met, you now must see whether your assumption of unlimited resources has overloaded your available resources.

Normally, you will find that you have people double- and triple-scheduled, which clearly won't work. These kinds of resource overloads can be resolved only by using computer software, except for very simple schedules. This is where the software really excels, and yet estimates are that only a few percent of all the people who purchase software actually use it to level resources.

Consider the small schedule in Figure 8-5. It contains only four tasks. Two are critical, and two have float. Task A requires two workers if it is to be completed in three weeks, and tasks B and C need one person each. When it comes time to do the proj-

Figure 8-5. Schedule with resources overloaded.

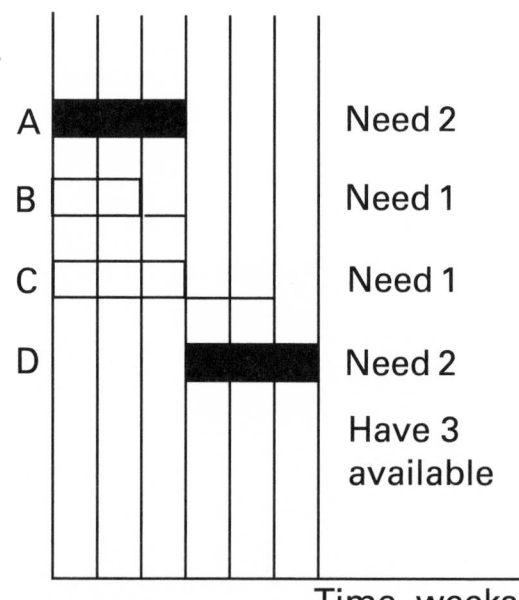

ect, however, you find that there are only three workers available. How did this happen?

It is possible that no more than three people were ever available, but because you followed the rule to schedule in parallel tasks that could logically be done in parallel, you inevitably overloaded your people. It is also possible that, when the plan was constructed, four workers were available but that one has since been assigned to another job that has priority over yours.

Whatever the reason, this schedule won't work unless something is changed. There are a number of possibilities. There are three areas to examine. You should first see whether any task has enough float to allow it to be delayed until resources become available. In this particular example, it turns out that this is possible. The solution is shown in Figure 8-6.

Of course, this solution is a nice textbook example that just happens to work out. It is never so easy in a real project. Notice

Figure 8-6. Schedule using float to level resources.

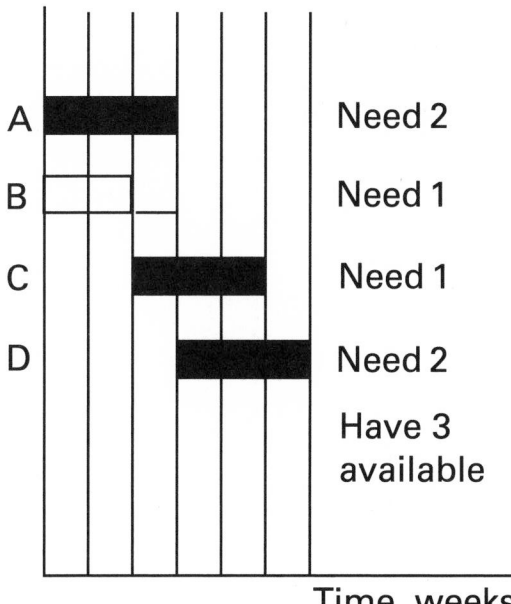

that task C has enough float that it can slide over and wait until activity B is finished. But what usually happens is that task C runs out of float before B is completed. Also, assume that task D needs three people, rather than two. As you can see, this complicates the situation considerably. This is shown in Figure 8-7.

Since this is the typical situation, we must be prepared to handle it. There are two more places to look for help. The first is the functional relationship among the variables:

$$C = f(P, T, S)$$

You should ask whether you can reduce scope, change the time limit, or reduce performance. Usually, performance is not negotiable, but the others may be. For example, sometimes you can reduce scope, and the project deliverable will still be acceptable to the client. Of course, if you can get another person for a short

Figure 8-7. Schedule with inadequate float on C to permit leveling.

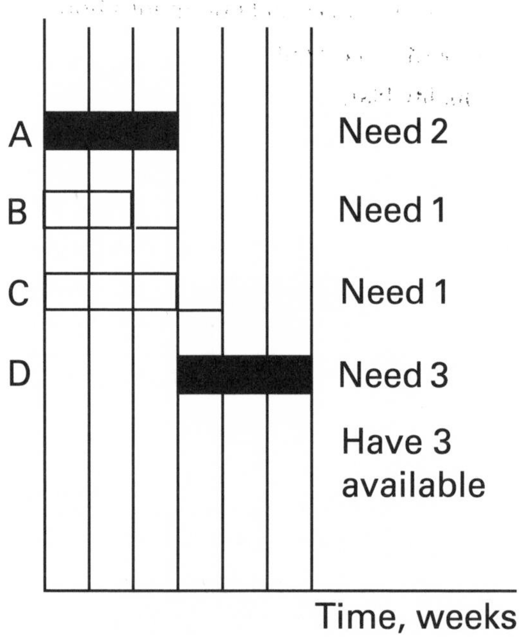

A   Need 2

B   Need 1

C   Need 1

D   Need 3

Have 3 available

Time, weeks

time, you won't have to consider reducing scope or performance. So you go shopping.

You ask the manager who "owns" the resources whether she can provide another person. She says sadly that she cannot and that she was even considering trying to take back another of the three she has already given you. Somehow you convince her not to do this. You then ask the project sponsor if it is okay to reduce scope. It is not.

It is also not okay to reduce performance. Nor can you find a contract employee in time to do the job. You are between a rock and a hard place. So you now ask whether there is another process that could be used to do the work. For example, if you can spray-paint a wall instead of using a roller, it may go much faster.

Suppose you try this and again you come up empty-handed. You decide the only thing left to do is resign your job. You never really wanted to be a project manager, anyway. But wait. Perhaps there is something else you can do.

Think back to what I said earlier. You use up all the float on C, and it is now a critical-path task. When you tell your software to level resources, it wants to know whether you want to schedule within the available float (or slack, as it is also called). If you say "yes," as soon as a task runs out of float, it won't move over any further. This is also called *time-critical resource leveling*, because time is of the essence for your project. (It always is!)

However, suppose you answer "no" to the question "Do you want to level within the available slack?" In this case, you are telling the software to continue sliding tasks over until resources become available, even if it means slipping the end date. (This is called *resource-critical leveling*.) When you try this with our example schedule, you arrive at the solution shown in Figure 8-8. Not bad, unless you can't live with the slip.

In fact, sometimes the slip is so bad that it seems almost ridiculous. Your project was originally going to end in December of the current year. Now the software says it is so starved for resources that it will end in the year 2013! Ridiculous! What good is a schedule that goes out that far?

Figure 8-8. Schedule under resource-critical conditions.

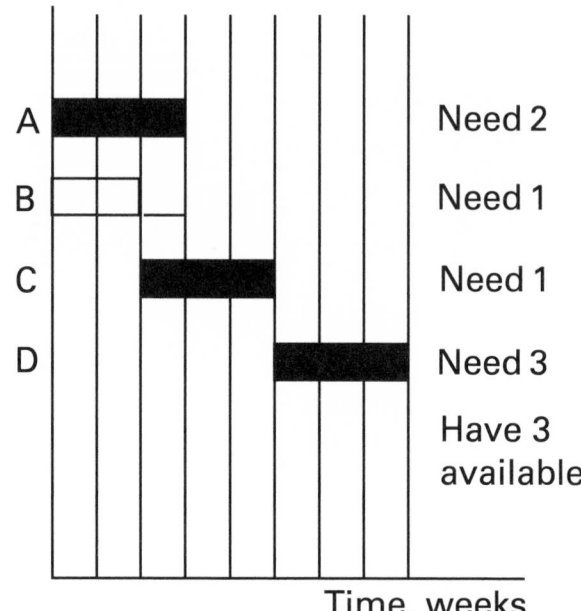

It can be used to bring the issue to everyone's attention. It shows the impact of inadequate resources and forces a trade-off as described earlier—that is, if everyone believes your schedule in the first place. I have just had an experience with a fellow who said that he didn't believe the schedules in the first place because he thought they were always unrealistic, so an unrealistic schedule subjected to fancy calculations didn't prove anything to him.

I'm sure that's true. However, if people are willing to accept the limitations of what we are doing when we plan a project, this is at least a way of showing the limitations you face. Everyone must understand that estimating is *guessing*, as is true of market and weather forecasting, neither of which has a stellar record. Moreover, all activities are subject to variation, as I have pointed out. If people don't understand this, then I suggest you turn in your project manager's hat for a better job.

Resource Availability

A major factor in dealing with resource allocation is the availability of each person to do project work. One guideline that industrial engineers follow is that no person is available to work more than 80 percent of the time. If you assume an eight-hour day, that means 6.4 hours a day available for work, and prudence says to just make it six hours. The 20 percent lost availability goes to three factors called PFD. P means personal—every individual must take breaks. F is for fatigue—you lose productive time as people get tired. And D means delays—people lose time waiting for inputs from others, supplies, or instructions on what to do.

Experience shows, however, that the only people who are available to work even 80 percent of the time are those whose jobs tie them to their work stations. This is true for factory workers and others who do routine jobs like processing insurance claims (and even these people move around). With knowledge workers, you never get 80 percent of a day in productive work. The figure is usually closer to 50 percent, and it may be lower! One company that I know of did a time study in which people logged their time every hour for two weeks, and they found that project work accounted for only 25 percent of their time. The rest went to meetings, nonproject work that had to be done, old jobs that were finished long ago but came back to the person who originally worked on them, work on budgets for the next year, customer support, and on and on.

Most software programs allow you to specify the number of *working hours* needed for a task and the percentage of a day that a person will work on the task; the software then translates those estimates into calendar time. So, as an example, if a person is working on your project only half time and the task she is doing is supposed to take twenty hours of actual working time, then it will be a week (or more) before she finishes it.

It is especially important that you know the availability of people to do project work, or you will produce schedules that are worse than useless. I say worse, because they will be misleadingly short, and they will wreak havoc with your organization. Do a time study to determine the number, then use it. And if people don't like the fact that a lot of time is being lost to nonproject activities, then correct the problem by removing those disruptive activities.

The usual solution is that people must work overtime to get their project work done because of all the disruptions that occur during the day. The problem is that studies have found that overtime has a very negative impact on productivity. So it is a losing battle. Short-term overtime is fine, but long spans just get organizations into trouble.

* *

Key Points to Remember

▶ You should ignore resource limitations when you begin developing a schedule. If two tasks can logically be done in parallel, draw them that way.

▶ The critical path is the one that is longest and has no float. Note that you can have a project on which the task with the longest path is not critical because it has float.

▶ Nobody is available to do productive work more than 80 percent of a workday. You lose 20 percent to personal time, fatigue, and delays.

* *

Exercise . . . .

For the network in Figure 8-9, calculate the early and late times and the float available on noncritical activities. Which activities form the critical path? Answers are in the Answers section at the back of the book.

Figure 8-9. Network for exercise.

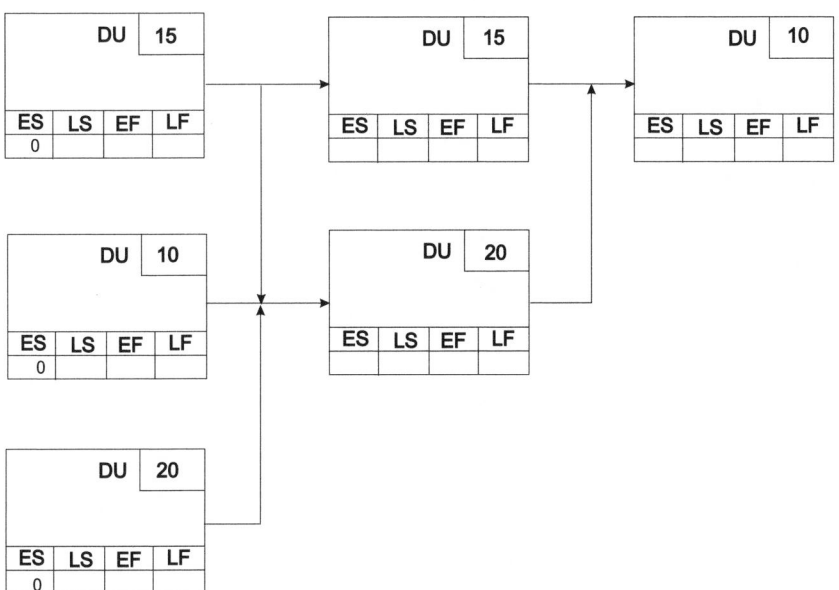

CHAPTER 9

Project Control and Evaluation

E very step taken up to now has been for one purpose—to achieve control of the project. This is what is expected of a project manager—that she manage organization resources in such a way that critical results are achieved.

However, there are two connotations to the word "control," and it is important that we use the one that is appropriate in today's world. One meaning of "control" refers to domination, power, command. We control people and things through the use of that power. When we say "Jump," people ask, "How high?" At least they used to. It doesn't work that well today.

I have previously discussed the fact that project managers often have a lot of responsibility but little authority. Let's examine that and see whether it is really a problem.

I have asked several corporate officers (presidents and vice presidents), "Since you have a lot of authority, does that authority guarantee that people will do what you want done?"

Uniformly, they answer, "No."

"What does get them to do what you want done?"

"Well, in the end analysis, they have to want to do it," they say.

"Then what does your authority do for you?" I ask.

"Well, it gives me the right to exercise sanctions over them, but that's all."

So we find that having authority is no guarantee that you will be able to get people to do your bidding. In the end, you have to get them to do it willingly, and that says you have to understand the motivations of people so that you can *influence* them to do what needs to be done.

> **There are two kinds of authority: One is power over people, and the other is the ability to make decisions and to act unilaterally.**

A second kind of authority has to do with taking actions unilaterally—that is, without having to get permission first. In this sense of the word, we *do* have a lot of organizational problems. I meet project managers who have project budgets in the millions of dollars (as much as $35 million in one case), yet who must have *all* expenditures approved. If a project plan and budget have been approved before the work was started and if the project manager is spending within the approved limits of the plan, why should she have to get more signatures for approved expenditures? Only if a deviation from the plan is going to result should more signatures be needed, and then the plan should be revised to reflect those changes.

Consider the messages being sent to these managers. On the one hand, they are being told, "We trust you to administer $35 million of our money." On the other hand, they are told, "But when you spend it, you must have every expenditure approved by someone of higher authority." One is a positive message: We trust you. The other is negative. Which do you think comes through loud and clear? You bet! The negative.

> **A *negative* message always takes priority over a positive one.**

Interestingly, we complain that people in organizations won't take more responsibility for themselves; then we treat them as though they are irresponsible and wonder why they don't behave responsibly!

So the first meaning of "control" has a power connotation. Another meaning is summed up by the highlighted definition. This definition was introduced in an earlier chapter. *Control* is the act of comparing progress to plan so that corrective action can be taken when a deviation from planned performance occurs. This definition implies the use of information as the primary ingredient of control, rather than power. Thus, we talk about management information systems, and, indeed, these are the essence of what is needed to achieve control in projects.

> **con•trol: to compare progress against plan so that corrective action can be taken when a deviation occurs**

Unfortunately, many organizations have management information systems that are good for tracking inventory, sales, and manufacturing labor but not for tracking projects. Where such systems are not in place, you will have to track progress manually.

Achieving Team Member Self-Control

Ultimately, the only way to control a project is for every member of the project team to be in control of his own work. A project manager can achieve control at the *macro* level only if it is achieved at the *micro* level. However, this does not mean that you should practice micromanaging! It actually means that you should set up conditions under which every team member can achieve control of his own efforts.

To do this requires five basic conditions. To achieve self-control, team members need:

1. A clear definition of what they are supposed to be doing, with the purpose stated

2. A personal plan for how to do the required work

3. Skills and resources adequate to the task

4. Feedback on progress that comes directly from the work itself

5. A clear definition of their authority to take corrective action when there is a deviation from plan (and it cannot be zero!)

The first requirement is that every team member be clear about what her objective is. Note the difference between tasks and objectives, which was discussed in Chapter 4. State the objective and explain to the person (if necessary) what the *purpose* of the objective is. This allows the individual to pursue the objective in her own way.

The second requirement is for every team member to have a personal plan on how to do the required work. Remember, if you have no plan, you have no control. This must apply at the individual, as well as at the overall, project level.

The third requirement is that the person have the skills and resources needed for the job. The need for resources is obvious, but this condition suggests that the person may have to be given training if she is lacking necessary skills. Certainly, when no employee is available with the required skills, it may be necessary to have team members trained.

The fourth requirement is that the person receive feedback on performance that goes directly to her. If such feedback goes through some roundabout way, she cannot exercise self-control. To make this clear, if a team member is building a wall, she must be able to measure the height of the wall, compare it to the planned performance, and know whether she is on track.

The fifth condition is that the individual must have a clear definition of her authority to take corrective action when there is a deviation from plan, and it must be greater than zero authority! If she has to ask the project manager what to do every time a deviation occurs, the project manager is still controlling. Furthermore, if many people have to seek approval for every minor action, this puts a real burden on the project manager.

Characteristics of a Project Control System

The control system must focus on project objectives, with the aim of ensuring that the project mission is achieved. To do that, the control system should be designed with these questions in mind:

▶ What is important to the organization?

▶ What are we attempting to do?

▶ Which aspects of the work are most important to track and control?

▶ What are the critical points in the process at which controls should be placed?

Control should be exercised over what is important. On the other hand, what is controlled tends to become important. Thus, if budgets and schedules are emphasized to the exclusion of quality, only those will be controlled. The project may well come in on time and within budget, but at the expense of quality. Project managers must monitor performance carefully to ensure that quality does not suffer.

Taking Corrective Action

A control system should focus on response—if control data do not result in action, then the system is ineffective. That is, if a control system does not use deviation data to *initiate corrective action*, it is not really a control system but simply a monitoring system. If you are driving and realize that you have somehow gotten on the wrong road but do nothing to get back on the right road, you are not exercising control.

One caution here, though. I once knew a manager whose response to a deviation was to go into the panic mode and begin micromanaging. He then got in the way of people trying to solve the problem and actually slowed them down. Had he left them alone, they would have solved their problem much faster.

Timeliness of Response

The response to control data must be timely. If action occurs too late, it will be ineffective. This is frequently a serious problem. Data on project status are sometimes delayed by four to six weeks, making them useless as a basis for taking corrective action. Ideally, information on project status should be available on a real-time basis. In most cases, that is not possible. For many projects, status reports that are prepared weekly are adequate.

Ultimately, you want to find out how many hours people *actually* work on your project and compare that figure to what was *planned* for them. This means that you want accurate data. In some cases, people fill out weekly time reports without having written down their working times daily. That results in a bunch of fiction, since most of us cannot remember with any accuracy what we did a week ago.

When people fill out time reports weekly, without writing down what they did daily, they are making up fiction. Such made-up data are almost worse than no data at all.

As difficult as it may be to do, you need to get people to record their working times daily so that the data will mean something when you collect them. What's in it for them? Perhaps nothing. Perhaps future estimates will be better as a result of your having collected accurate information on this project. In any case, you need accurate data, or you may as well not waste your time collecting them.

When information collection is delayed for too long, the manager may end up making things worse, instead of better. Lags in feedback systems are a favorite topic for systems theorists. The government's attempts to control recessions and inflation sometimes involve long delays, as a result of which the government winds up doing the exact opposite of what should have been done, thereby making the economic situation worse.

There is one point about control that is important to note. If every member of the project team is practicing proper control methods, then reports that are prepared weekly are just checks and balances. This is the desired condition.

Designing the Right System

One control system is not likely to be correct for all projects. It may need to be scaled down for small projects and beefed up for large ones. Generally, a control system adequate for a large project will overwhelm a small one with paperwork, while one that is good for small projects won't have enough clout for a big project.

Practicing the KISS Principle

KISS stands for "Keep it simple, stupid!" The smallest control effort that achieves the desired result should be used. Any control data that are not essential should be eliminated. However, as was just mentioned, one common mistake is to try to control complex projects with systems that are *too simple!*

> No problem is so big or so complicated that it can't be run away from.
>
> —Charlie Brown (Charles Schultz, Peanuts)

To keep control simple, it is a good idea to check periodically that reports that are generated are actually being used for something by the people who receive them. We sometimes create reports because we believe the information in them should be useful to others, but if the recipients don't actually use it, we are kidding ourselves. To test this point, send a memo with each report telling people to let you know whether they want to receive future reports; if you do not hear from them, their names will be removed from the distribution. You may be surprised to find that *no one* uses some of your reports. Those reports should be dropped completely.

Project Review Meetings

There are two aspects to project control. One can be called *maintenance*, and the other aims at *improvement* of performance. The maintenance review just tries to keep the project on track. The improvement review tries to help project teams improve performance. Three kinds of reviews are routinely conducted to achieve these purposes. They are:

1. Status reviews

2. Process or lessons-learned reviews

3. Design reviews

Everyone should do status and process reviews. Design reviews, of course, are appropriate only if you are designing hardware, software, or some sort of campaign, such as a marketing campaign.

A status review is aimed at maintenance. It asks where the project stands on the PCTS measures that we have used throughout this book. Only if you know the value of all four of these can you be sure where you are. This is the subject of Chapter 11.

Process means the way something is done, and you can be sure that process always affects task performance. That is, how something is done affects the outcome. For that reason, process improvement is the work of every manager. How this is done is covered in the next section.

Project Evaluation

As the dictionary definition says, to evaluate a project is to attempt to determine whether the overall status of the work is acceptable, in terms of intended value to the client once the job is finished. Project evaluation appraises the progress and performance of a job and compares them to what was originally planned. That evaluation provides the basis for management decisions on how to proceed with the project. The evaluation must be credible in the eyes of everyone affected, or decisions based on it will not

e•val•u•ate: to determine or judge the value or worth of

—*The Random House Dictionary*

be considered valid. The primary tool for project evaluation is the *project process review*, which is usually conducted at major milestones throughout the life of the project.

Purposes of Project Evaluation

Sports teams that practice without reviewing performance may get really *good* at playing very *badly*. That is why they review game films—to see where they need to improve. In other words, the purpose of a review is to learn lessons that can help the team to avoid doing things that cause undesired outcomes and to continue doing those that help. The review should be called a *lessons-learned* or *process* review.

I have deliberately avoided the word *audit*, because nobody likes to be audited. Historically, an audit has been designed to catch people doing things they shouldn't have done so that they can be penalized in some way. If you go around auditing people, you can be sure they will hide from you anything they don't want you to know, and it is those very things that could help the company learn and grow.

As Dr. W. Edwards Deming has pointed out, there are two kinds of organizations in this world today—those that are getting better and those that are dying. An organization that stands still is dying. It just doesn't know it yet.

The reason? The competition is not sitting by idly. It is doing new things, some of which may be better than what you are doing. If you aren't improving, you will be passed by, and soon you won't have a market.

The same is true of every part of an organization. You can't suboptimize, improving just manufacturing. You have to improve every department, and that includes how you run projects.

> **Good management of projects can give you a competitive advantage.**

In fact, good project management can give you a real competitive advantage, especially in product development. If you are sloppy in managing your projects, you don't have good control of development costs. That means that you have to either sell a lot of product or charge large margins to cover your development costs so that the project is worth doing in the first place. If you can't sell a lot of widgets, then you have to charge the large margin.

If your competitor, on the other hand, has good cost control, it can charge smaller margins and still be sure that it recovers its investment and makes money. Thus, it has a competitive advantage over you because of its better *control* of project work.

Additionally, in order to learn, people require feedback, like that gained by a team from reviewing game films. The last phase of a project should be a final process review, conducted so that the management of projects can be improved. However, such a process review should not be conducted only at the end of the project. Rather, process reviews should be done at major milestones in the project or every three months, whichever comes first, so that learning can take place as the job progresses. Furthermore, if a project is getting into serious trouble, the process review should reveal the difficulty so that a decision can be made to continue or terminate the work.

> **In order to learn, we must have feedback. Furthermore, we tend to learn more from mistakes than from successes, painful though that may be to admit.**

Following are some of the general reasons for conducting periodic project process reviews. You should be able to:

► Improve project performance together with the management of the project.

► Ensure that quality of project work does not take a back seat to schedule and cost concerns.

► Reveal developing problems early so that action can be taken to deal with them.

► Identify areas where other projects (current or future) should be managed differently.

▶ Keep client(s) informed of project status. This can also help ensure that the completed project will meet the needs of the client.

▶ Reaffirm the organization's commitment to the project for the benefit of project team members.

Conducting the Project Process Review

Ideally, a project process review should be conducted by an independent examiner, who can remain objective in the assessment of information. However, the process review must be conducted in a spirit of learning, rather than in a climate of blame and punishment. If people are afraid that they will be "strung up" for problems, then they will hide those problems if at all possible.

Even so, openness is hard to achieve. In many organizations, the climate has been punitive for so long that people are reluctant to reveal any less-than-perfect aspects of project performance. Dr. Chris Argyris, in his book *Overcoming Organizational Defenses: Facilitating Organization Learning*, has described the processes by which organizations continue ineffective practices. All of them are intended to help individuals "save face" or avoid embarrassment. In the end, they also prevent organizational learning.

Process reviews conducted as witch-hunts will produce witches.

Two questions should be asked in the review. The first is "What have we done well so far?," and the second is "What do we want to improve (or do better) in the future?" Notice that I am not asking "What have we done badly?" That question serves only to make everyone defensive, because people will assume that you will punish them for things done wrong. Furthermore, there is always the possibility that nothing has been done wrong, but there is always room to improve.

Finally, the results of the review should be published. Otherwise, the only people in the organization who can take advantage of it are the members of the team just reviewed. If other teams know what was learned, then they can benefit from that information. In the next section, we look at what the report should contain.

The Process Review Report

A company may decide to conduct process reviews in varying degrees of thoroughness, from totally comprehensive, to partial, to less formal and cursory. A formal, comprehensive process review should be followed by a report. The report should contain as a minimum the following:

▶ *Current project status.* The best way to do this is to use earned value analysis, as presented in Chapter 11. However, when earned value analysis is not used, the current status should still be reported as accurately as possible.

▶ *Future status.* This is a forecast of what is expected to happen in the project. Are significant deviations expected in schedule, cost, performance, or scope? If so, the report should specify the nature of the changes.

▶ *Status of critical tasks.* The report should describe the status of critical tasks, particularly those on the critical path. Tasks that have high levels of technical risk should be given special attention, as should those being performed by outside vendors or subcontractors, over which the project manager may have limited control.

▶ *Risk assessment.* The report should mention any identified risks that could lead to monetary loss, project failure, or other liabilities.

▶ *Information relevant to other projects.* The report should describe what has been learned from this process review that can or should be applied to other projects, whether in progress or about to start.

▶ *Limitations of the process review.* The report should mention any factors that may limit the validity of the process review.

Are any assumptions suspect? Are any data missing or perhaps contaminated? Was anyone uncooperative in providing information for the process review?

As a general comment, the simpler and more straightforward a project process review report, the better. The information should be organized so that both planned and actual results can be easily compared. Significant deviations should be highlighted and explained.

Key Points to Remember

▶ The meaning of control that is important to project managers is the one that concerns the use of information, comparing actual progress to the plan so that action can be taken to correct for deviations from plan.

▶ The only way a project is really in control is if all team members are in control of their own work.

▶ The effort used to control a project should be worthwhile. You don't want to spend $100 to purchase a $3 battery, for example.

▶ If you take no action in response to a deviation, you have a *monitoring* system, not a *control* system.

▶ Project working times must be recorded daily. If people wait a week to capture what they have done, they rely on memory and end up writing down *estimates* of what they did. Such data are no good for future estimating.

▶ Project evaluation is done to determine whether a project should continue or be canceled. Process reviews also should help the team learn in order to improve performance.

CHAPTER 10

The Change Control Process

T he most comprehensive, effective project plan will be wasted if some method of controlling change is not implemented. Just as your diligence and ability to invest in planning directly affect project success or failure, so too does the establishment of a change control process. The *PMBOK® Guide* addresses the change process, stating, "When issues are found while project work is being performed, change requests are issued which may modify project policies or procedures, project scope, project cost or budget, project schedule, or project quality." If you do not keep the plan current, you have no plan. The original baseline plan (the foundation) will no longer be valid and will lose its effectiveness in dealing with current project scenarios.

Change control is not easy. It involves variables and judgment calls, thresholds and signoffs. The change control process establishes the stability necessary for you to manage the multitude of changes that

The change control process establishes the stability necessary for you to manage the multitude of changes that affect the project throughout its life cycle.

affect the project throughout its life cycle. If left unchecked, changes to the project plan cause significant imbalance regarding scope, schedule, and budget. The project manager who focuses on managing and controlling change develops a potent weapon to fight scope creep (see Chapter 3). As changes occur, you will gain the ability to gauge their overall impact on the project and react accordingly.

Change control cannot be accomplished in a vacuum. As you react and make adjustments, the project plan must be revised and distributed to predetermined stakeholders. These stakeholders are often identified in a project communication plan. In addition to stakeholder identification, the plan determines appropriate communication paths, levels of data dissemination, and general guidelines or protocols for the project team. This is an excellent example of how different elements of an overall project plan can complement each other. Typical stakeholders that should appear on the *inform* or *distribution* list are the project champion, team members, functional managers, support personnel, select external vendors, and legal. There can be other stakeholders involved as the project dictates.

Sources of Change

Change happens. As things mature and grow, changes occur naturally and are often healthy and welcome. Projects are no different. Issues arise, however, when changes occur and no corresponding assessment is made of their impact on the project, positive or negative. Sources of change can be many and varied, depending on the project. Think about the projects you are working on right now. What has caused you to modify your plan or make adjustments? With some projects, the customer or an internal department may be driving the modifications. On others, changes can come from all possible directions. Figure 10-1 presents a visual illustration of this concept.

As you can see, each side of the *triple constraints triangle* represents a key project constraint. Sources of change are gener-

Figure 10-1. Triple constraints triangle.

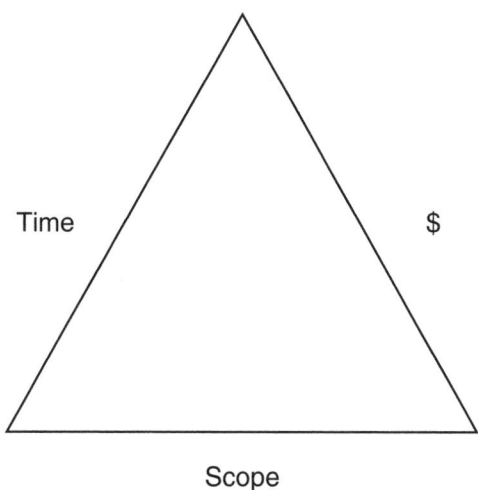

Scope

ally associated with one or more sides of the triangle: scope, schedule, or budget. Project quality is a constant and should always be considered as a potential source and focus of change control. Scope changes should be identified as those that affect the project deliverable. As changes hit the triangle, it is your job to keep the triangle balanced by making necessary adjustments to your plan. If this is not accomplished, one or more sides of the triangle will become skewed and therefore imbalanced. Extra work will be required to complete the project successfully. Typical sources per the triangle include, but are not limited to:

> **Sources of change are generally associated with one or more sides of the triangle: scope, schedule, or budget.**

Scope

▶ Other projects are added due to consolidation

▶ The client changes the requirements

▶ Market conditions shift

▶ Problems encountered by engineering

Schedule

▶ Delivery date accelerated

▶ Competition pressures

▶ Client requests early delivery

Budget

▶ Management pulls 20 percent of the project budget

▶ Raw material costs escalate

▶ Project work requires the addition of a team member

Understanding and identifying likely sources of change to your projects will assist you in remaining proactive. The change control process will require a decision as to whether or not to process the change request and then determine the most effective way to move forward. Some decisions are easy: the customer requests a legitimate design improvement or the project champion de-prioritizes the project and slips required delivery three months. But project fate dictates that many change requests require difficult assessments, analyses, and various approvals before the change can be processed. It is not always evident whether a specific change adds value or merely cosmetic adjustments to the project plan. The formal change control process really is your friend. As you will see in the next section, it helps guide you through the gray areas of change that often develop as the project matures.

The Six Steps in the Change Control Process

The change control process can vary but usually includes a number of important and mandatory steps. In this section I outline six common steps that are found in a typical project change control process. Organizational culture, procedure, and project type directly affect how the steps are implemented. The project manager typically receives a change request from the requesting *entity* (individual/department/customer). At this point, it is important that you confirm the current version of the project plan. If the change is processed, its impact will be measured against the plan and adjustments made accordingly. *Keep the baseline current.*

Step 1: Enter initial change control information into your change control log.

Entering initial change control information into your change control log serves as the summary of all actions taken regarding changes requested and/or processed. A detailed change log can ultimately serve as a biography of the project as it matures (see Figure 10-3 on page 136).

Step 2: Determine if the change should be processed.

By determining if the change should be processed, you take on the role of the project's gatekeeper. All too often, I have seen project managers accept changes simply because they are requested. If the change doesn't make sense—if it doesn't add value or should not be processed for other reasons—push back. Request clarification or justification to help you arrive at a reasonable decision. If the change is rejected, log it and stop the process. If the change is accepted, begin assessing the impact to the project plan. This is typically done by asking this question: *"How does the change affect the sides of my triangle: scope, schedule, and budget?"*

Quality, objective, and other elements of the project should also be considered when assessing impact. Prepare recommendations for implementation and then complete the change control form.

Step 3: Submit recommendations to management and/or the customer for review and approval.

Recommendations for review and approval should be submitted to management and/or your customer, including those for impact assessment. Other approvals should be obtained as necessary (i.e., functional department managers). Make appropriate modifications as comments are received from these stakeholders.

Step 4: Update the project plan.

Don't forget to update the project plan! This can be and sometimes is forgotten in the frantic pace of the project environment. It is here that you will create a new project baseline. This will become the *current* plan.

Step 5: Distribute the updated plan.

As previously mentioned, communication when the updated plan is distributed is critical. You use this step to ensure that all stakeholders are aware of the change and the adjusted baseline plan (for instance, revision 7). If the distribution list is incomplete, misalignment will occur between the project team and one or more of the stakeholders. Imagine your project team working on revision 3 while the California office is working on the original plan (this is actually a bad memory for me).

Step 6: Monitor the change and track progress against the revised plan.

The impact of the change activity may be minor or severe, good or bad. Don't forget to check the project triangle to ensure that it remains balanced.

Organizational culture impacts how you establish the change control process and manage changes to your project. Be flexible. I often ask my seminar attendees if they have an existing change control process to guide them; some do, but most don't. That reflects my own experience. When I moved from the defense industry (strong project processes) to the adult learning environment (less process), I needed to adjust. If you are faced with an environment where there are no change processes in place, that is a good news, bad news scenario. The difficulty is in establishing change control while facing resistance to change, as well as general apathy. Nobody wants to sign anything, and there is little support in the decision-making process. Do it anyway! It is important for you to maintain control of the project through these changes. If a stakeholder or department manager signature cannot be obtained, write the department or stakeholder/manager name on the change control form and note the date. This is a control mechanism, not a "gotcha." As project manager, it is your responsibility to fight scope creep and keep the triple constraints triangle balanced and under control. This is *your* tool for *your* project. The good news in the absence of any process is the absence of any process. You can set this up any way you like because there is nothing to replace. Yes, this will be time consuming and a lot of work, but the payoff will be your process, your style.

For those who work in an environment with established change control procedures, use them. Quite often these procedures are designed to manage changes to the *product* (IT, R & D departments), not the project. Make sure you take a holistic approach to change and focus on the project itself.

The Change Control Form

The change control form is the controlling document for the change process. This document is the project manager's tool for identifying, assessing, and, if necessary, processing changes that affect the project. In short, it keeps the project plan current. It should be filled out completely upon acceptance of the requested change. The data input is more than record keeping and requires analysis, estimation, and collaboration with team members, stakeholders, and subject matter experts. Without this form or a close proximity, there is no process because there is no control.

> **The change control form is the controlling document for the change process.**

Figure 10-2. Project change control form.

Project Title: Moving Relocation Project   **Date:** 8/12/2011

Project No.: 710   **Task No.:** 16   **Revision No.:** 1   **Date Revised:** 8/13/2011

Objective Statement:
Relocation of the accounting department to suitable and renovated quarters for 22 persons within the same building no later than December 31, 2011.

Description of Change:
Site #2 will not be available for evaluation until August 21 or 22. This will cause a two-day delay in the evaluation of all sites. This change will probably not cause a delay to the project but may delay the final site decision by one day.

Reason for Change:
The site will not be available for review and evaluation due to major corporate planning sessions that will consume that space for two days.

Schedule Change Information

Task No.	Task	Orig. Start Date	Orig. Comp. Date	New Start Date	New Comp. Date
16	Evaluate Site #2	8/15/11	8/20/11	8/17/11	8/22/11

Estimated Costs:

Approvals

Project Manager: Mr. Bill Boyd	**Date:** 8/11/11
Task Manager: Mr. Dan O'Brien	**Date:** 8/12/11
Functional Manager:	**Date:**
Senior Manager:	**Date:**

Figure 10-2 is a very comprehensive, detailed version of a change form. It is important that you review the form and adjust it to your own perceived requirements when managing changes as the project matures. You may need to streamline the template, or you may want to expand some portions. This is your call. If the document is too cumbersome, you will lose efficiency. If you simplify too much, key data will be lost.

Overview data are input at the top of the form, including project number, revision number, and date revised. I *always* include the objective statement on my change documents to ensure continuity and eliminate uncertainty. Change can breed uncertainty, and uncertainty is not your friend. As changes multiply on a typical project, include the original objective statement. This will keep stakeholders from wondering if the objective has changed because of the latest adjustments. If the impact is significant, a new objective statement may need to be agreed upon and communicated per the form. A brief description of the change is appropriate, and the reason should be included, as well. In the mercurial project environment, it may be difficult seven months and thirty-seven changes into the project to recall why the team generated change order Number 2. Add the five other projects you might be managing to the scenario, and you can see how this added element of control can be helpful. *Reason for change* can also serve as a check on the system to ensure that value is added by implementing the change.

Schedule change information and estimated costs bring us back to the triple constraints triangle. It is crucial that you quantify the estimated impact of the change on both the project schedule and the budget. Some project managers prefer less detail than is shown in Figure 10–2 and quantify the impact by noting the overall schedule delay or time saved. This is your call and is usually determined by style, organizational culture, project type, and so on. Sometimes, estimated costs are actual costs already realized or quotes received from vendors. Again, this will depend upon all of the variables associated with the change.

An effective change control form is obviously important for project control, but it can also come in handy:

A colleague of mine, a group program manager for the American Management Association International (AMA), was asked by a direct report managing a course revision project if she could colorize 25 percent of a *Train the Trainer* course book. He told her it was probably not a good idea because the production costs would be exorbitant. When she brought back a more reasonable request with appropriate approvals, the manager moved forward with the change, impacting the budget by about $10,000. At the subsequent steering committee review, he was asked about the budget increase. Expecting the question, he offered his next slide, a copy of the change request form, which two of the committee members had signed. He was able to proceed without needing an aspirin.

Thresholds

How much change is enough to trigger the process? Are there changes that are just not significant enough to justify filling out the form, acquiring signatures, and making other investments of time and effort? These are important questions for the project manager, and they offer an excellent time to consider thresholds. Most project processes require you to employ good project and business savvy. If the change is considered minor and the project plan can absorb the change with minimal impact, make necessary adjustments and move on (see Example 1). If, however, a severity threshold has been exceeded, this should trigger action by you and your team to implement the change control process (see Example 2).

> **Are there changes that are just not significant enough to justify filling out the form, acquiring signatures, and making other investments of time and effort?**

Example 1: If a $5 million project must endure a $10 change, it would be a poor decision to trigger the process. A reasonable threshold might be $500, depending upon budget constraints and industry standards.

Example 2: If your project deadline is four months from the date of the change request and the estimated schedule delay is one week, the change process should be triggered. Schedule thresholds require more analysis based upon critical path implications (or not) and duration to complete. As always, you will need to take the temperature of the project environment during the decision-making process.

Because of the ever-changing environment that surrounds most projects, thresholds are flexible, and you will often require input from teammates or other stakeholders to determine the impact of a change on the project. If you have done your homework and invested time and effort in managing the previous project life-cycle processes, you will be in a much better position to make informed decisions regarding change.

The Change Control Log

As I mentioned earlier in this chapter, the change control log enters the picture in Step 1 of the change control process. As you might expect, it is another control mechanism designed to identify proposed changes and track those accepted throughout the process.

Figure 10-3 is a template that you can use as presented, streamline, or expand as you deem necessary. In the absence of an organizational standard, I recommend that you adopt a singular, comprehensive approach to tracking changes across projects. You can add or omit information as appropriate.

As with many project templates, the concept is simple but not

Figure 10-3. Project change control log.

Change Number	Date of Change	Description of Change	Requested By	Status O/C	Schedule Impact	Budget Impact	Comments
1	8/12/11	Site #2 not available on 2/11	Jim Morrison		2 days	N/A	

always easy to apply. Discipline is the key ingredient here. As changes, risks, and critical path issues are swirling about, you must be disciplined enough to stop what you are doing and work the log. Much of the information you input will seem self-evident or trivial, but the simplest detail may loom large as the project progresses. Change Number, Date of Change Request, and an abbreviated Description of Change are standard information. The approach used in Figure 10-3 also includes columns for the requestor and status. There will be instances where a change will be accepted but budget, schedule, technology, skill set, or something else presents a blockage to delay or even prevent implementation. I prefer O/C, open or closed,

> As changes, risks, and critical path issues are swirling about, you must be disciplined enough to stop what you are doing and work the log.

to identify status. You should then transfer Schedule Impact and Budget Impact from the change control form and update as necessary. Many project managers add a column for scope or objective impact prior to the final input that is reserved for comments or miscellaneous issues. Typical comments may concern stakeholder reluctance, technical problems, or remarks regarding other project issues.

The Project Spin-off

Think about some drastic changes that have affected your projects in the past. Sometimes project change, whatever the source, can be grounds for spinning off a new project while continuing with the original. Sometimes it is appropriate for the new project to simply replace the original due to skill set requirements, location, budget demands, deprioritization, or a host of other reasons. There are also changes so severe that they justify closing the project down. When you get hit with the big one, it's not often easy and never fun. It doesn't even need to be one change; it may be an accumulation of changes that dramatically impacts the project. In any case, you need to have a firm grasp of the impact on the project and your recommendations moving forward. This can often be a sales job, and you will need to persuade with good data from the project plan.

> Sometimes project change, whatever the source, can be grounds for spinning off a new project while continuing with the original.

The project spin-off usually occurs when the change is so dramatic that you and your team determine that an entirely separate project should be initiated. This could be due to scope "explosion" or one or more of the many reasons previously detailed. If a new project moves forward with the existing one, it can often be managed in parallel, requiring coordination and alignment. If a new project manager takes over, it is probable that you will be called upon to coach her up to speed as the project life cycle is begun. It is in

> The project spin-off usually occurs when the change is so dramatic that you and your team determine that an entirely separate project should be initiated.

your best interest to do a thorough job here. Some of your team resources may be shared or transferred, depending upon the individual project circumstances.

If the new project becomes a *satellite*, or subproject, the impact is far less drastic, and the new team will usually report directly to the original project manager. In contrast, if the new project replaces the old, you may just move on to other projects. In the event that it makes sense to keep you in place, manage the new project as you did the original. Begin at the beginning—*plan.* Then continue through the project life cycle as appropriate. It is important here to capture all of the work and data that can be useful moving forward on the new project. A careful analysis should be done to separate the wheat from the chaff. In some cases, skill-set requirements will require individual team members to be replaced. You may have to recruit an entirely new team, again depending on circumstances.

You may, as project manager, decide that the project should be *killed;* good luck. In my experience, it can be a difficult thing to do, but not impossible. If the project has lost its value, make your case. Use data, not emotion. The reasons can be many and varied, but if you have done your job, you will have the means to persuade with facts.

Embracing Change

Don't fear project change; embrace and manage it. This does not have to be a difficult task if you have invested yourself and the project team in establishing a formidable plan. As with scope creep, changes often represent necessary adjustments to the original project plan. It's how you manage these changes that makes all of the difference and helps you deliver the project on time and on budget, with an excellent deliverable.

●●●
Key Points to Remember

▶ Change must be controlled *and* communicated.

▶ Understanding and identifying likely sources of change assists you in remaining proactive. Typical sources of change are scope, schedule, and budget adjustments.

▶ It is crucial to keep the baseline plan current.

▶ The six common steps you will take in a typical change control process are to enter the initial change control information into your change control log; determine if the change should be processed; submit recommendations to management and/or the customer for review and approval; update the project plan; distribute the updated plan; and monitor the change and track progress against the revised plan.

▶ The change control form and log are your primary controlling documents.

▶ Thresholds should be established when determining your response to project change.

▶ Project spin-off usually occurs when the project change is so dramatic that you and your team determine that an entirely separate project should be initiated.
●●●

Exercise . . . .

Identify a recent change to your project that required a response. On the basis of what you've learned in this chapter, answer the following questions:

1. Is it appropriate to accept the change?

2. Should a change control document be triggered?

3. How did this change impact the project triangle?

4. To whom should the response be communicated?

5. What change thresholds are appropriate to establish for this project?

CHAPTER 11

Project Control Using Earned Value Analysis

C ontrol is exercised to achieve project objectives, and we know that there are performance, cost, time, and scope targets that are always important. Furthermore, we have seen that control is exercised by comparing performance to plan and, when deviations or *variances* occur, taking corrective action to bring performance back on target.

As I said in Chapter 9, the review that is concerned with maintenance or straightforward project control is the *status* review. This review asks where the project is in terms of all four PCTS variables. Each time progress is reviewed, you must ask these three questions:

1. Where are we (in terms of PCTS)?

2. When there is a deviation, what caused it?

3. What should be done about the deviation?

Note that there are only four actions that can be taken in response to question 3. These are:

1. Cancel the project.

2. Ignore the deviation.

3. Take corrective action to get back onto the planned progress.

4. Revise the plan to reflect a change in status that can't be corrected.

Sometimes a project gets so far off track that it is no longer viable, and the best thing to do is to cancel it. Of course, this step is not taken lightly, but it should be taken in cases where you are just going to throw good money after bad. Cut your losses and get on with something better.

As for ignoring a deviation, if you can control to within a certain percentage tolerance and you are within those limits, you should usually ignore a deviation unless it shows a trend that will definitely eventually take it outside the limits. Otherwise, tweaking may just make the situation worse.

As for taking corrective action, there is no way to tell what this means, as it is specific to each project. Sometimes working people overtime gets a project back on track. Or perhaps you need to add people, or cut scope, or change the process. You must determine what must be done for your project.

In the event that the project is still viable but nothing can be done to get it back on track, you may have to revise the plan. Of course, you can also consider working overtime or reducing scope, since these were not originally called for. What I am really referring to here, however, is a situation in which you cannot recover and you are revising the plan to show that the costs will increase, the deadline will slip, or some other change to the plan will occur.

> **Another day, another zero.**
>
> —Alfalfa (Carl Switzer)
> *Our Gang comedy series*

Measuring Progress

One of the hardest things to do in managing projects is to actually *measure* progress. When you are following a road map, you monitor the road signs and see whether they agree with your planned route. In well-defined jobs, such as construction projects, it is generally fairly easy to tell where you are. You can measure the height of a brick wall or see whether all the conduit is installed, and so on. That is, you can tell where you are when a part of the work is actually *finished*. When work is poorly defined and it is only partially complete, however, you have to *estimate* where you are.

This is especially true of knowledge work—work done with one's head, rather than one's hands. If you are writing software code, designing something, or writing a book, it can be very hard to judge how far along you are and how much you have left to do.

Naturally, if you can't tell where you are, you can't exercise control. And note that use of the word "estimate" in measuring progress. What exactly is an estimate?

It's a guess.

And so we are guessing about where we are.

Yes. We'll know where we are when we get there. Until we actually arrive, we're guessing.

Does this not sound like something from *Alice in Wonderland?*

Heavens.

What was that definition of control again? Let's see—compare where you are . . .

How do you know where you are . . .

We're guessing.

. . . against where you are supposed to be. . . .

How do you know where you're supposed to be?

Oh, that's much easier. The plan tells us.

But where did the plan come from?

It was an estimate, too.

Oh. So if one guess doesn't agree with the other guess, we're supposed to take corrective action to make the two of them agree, is that it?

That's what this guy says in his book.

Must be a book on witchcraft and magic.

Well, since it is impossible to know for sure where we are,

then perhaps we should just give up on the whole thing and keep running projects by the seat of the pants. Right?

Wrong.

The fact that measures of progress are not very accurate does not justify the conclusion that they shouldn't be used. Remember, if you have no plan, you have no control, and if you don't try to monitor and follow the plan, you definitely don't have control. And if you have no control, there is no semblance of managing. You're just flailing around.

> **The difficulty of measuring progress does not justify the conclusion that it shouldn't be done. You cannot have control unless you measure progress.**

What is important to note, however, is that some projects are capable of tighter control than others. Well-defined work, which can be accurately measured, can be controlled to tight tolerances. Work that is more nebulous (e.g., knowledge work) has to allow larger tolerances. Management must recognize this and accept it. Otherwise, you go crazy trying to achieve 3 percent tolerances. It's like trying to push a noodle into a straight line or nail jelly to a wall.

Measuring Project Performance/Quality

If you think measuring progress is hard, try measuring quality. Were the bolts holding the steel beams together put in properly? Are all the welds sound? How do you tell?

> **Work quality is most likely to be sacrificed when deadlines are tight. Constant attention is required to avoid this tendency.**

This is the hardest variable to track, and one that often suffers as a consequence. Also, so much attention tends to be focused on cost and schedule performance that the quality of the work is often sacrificed. This can be a disaster, in some cases resulting in lawsuits against a company for damages that result from poor-quality work.

Project managers must pay special attention to the quality variable, in spite of the difficulty of tracking it.

Earned Value Analysis

It is one thing to meet a project deadline at any cost. It is another to do it for a *reasonable* cost. Project cost control is concerned with ensuring that projects stay within their budgets, while getting the work done on time and at the correct quality.

One system for doing this, called *earned value analysis*, was developed in the 1960s to allow the government to decide whether a contractor should receive a progress payment for work done. The method is finally coming into its own outside government projects, and it is considered the correct way to monitor and control almost any project. The method is also called simply *variance analysis*.

Variance analysis allows the project manager to determine trouble spots in the project and to take corrective action. The following definitions are useful in understanding the analysis:

▶ *Cost variance*: Compares deviations and performed work.

▶ *Schedule variance*: Compares planned and actual work completed.

▶ *BCWS* (budgeted cost of work scheduled): The budgeted cost of work scheduled to be done in a given time period or the level of effort that is supposed to be performed in that period.

▶ *BCWP* (budgeted cost of work performed): The budgeted cost of work actually performed in a given period or the budgeted level of effort actually expended. BCWP is also called *earned value* and is a measure of the dollar value of the work actually accomplished in the period being monitored.

▶ *ACWP* (actual cost of work performed): The amount of money (or effort) actually spent in completing work in a given period.

Variance thresholds can be established that define the level at which reports must be sent to various levels of management within an organization.

$$\text{Cost Variance} = \text{BCWP} - \text{ACWP}$$
$$\text{Schedule Variance} = \text{BCWP} - \text{BCWS}$$
$$\text{Variance: Any deviation from plan}$$

By combining cost and schedule variances, an integrated cost/schedule reporting system can be developed.

Variance Analysis Using Spending Curves

Variances are often plotted using spending curves. A BCWS curve for a project is presented in Figure 11-1. It shows the *cumulative spending* planned for a project and is sometimes called a *baseline plan.*

In the event that software is not available to provide the necessary data, Figure 11-2 shows how data for the curve are generated. Consider a simple bar chart schedule. Only three tasks are involved. Task A involves forty labor-hours per week at an average loaded labor rate of $20 per hour, so that task costs $800 per week. Task B involves 100 hours per week of labor at $30 per hour, so it costs $3,000 per week. Finally, task C spends $2,400 per week, assuming sixty hours per week of labor at $40 per hour.

At the bottom of the chart, we see that during the first week $800 is spent for project labor; in the second week, both tasks A and B are running, so the labor expenditure is $3,800. In the third week, all three tasks are running, so labor expenditure is the sum of the three, or $6,200. These are the *weekly* expenditures.

The *cumulative* expenditures are calculated by adding the cost for each subsequent week to the previous cumulative total. These cumulative amounts are plotted in Figure 11-3. This is the spending curve for the project and is called a BCWS curve. Since

Figure 11-1. BCWS curve.

Cumulative Spending
Time

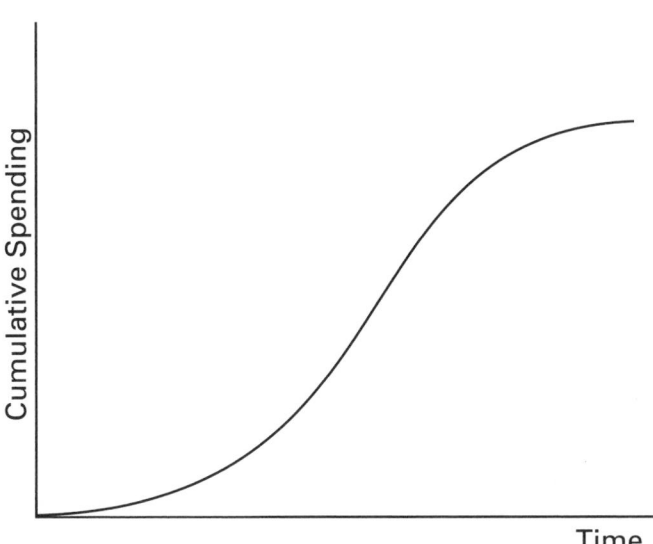

Figure 11-2. Bar chart schedule illustrating cumulative spending.

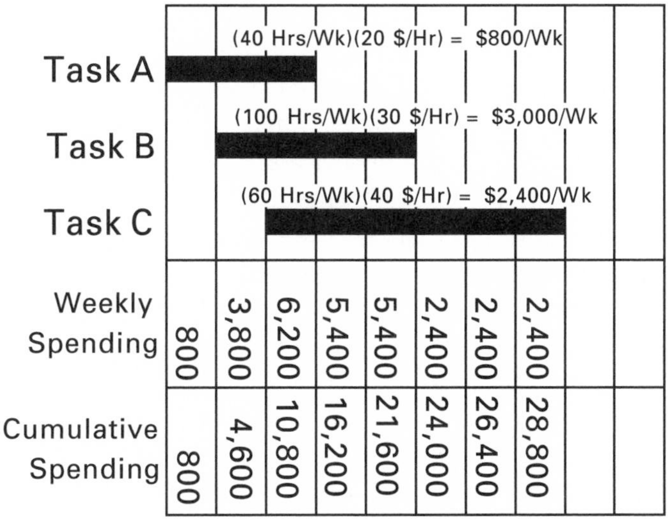

Task A
(40 Hrs/Wk)(20 $/Hr) = $800/Wk
Task B
(100 Hrs/Wk)(30 $/Hr) = $3,000/Wk
Task C
(60 Hrs/Wk)(40 $/Hr) = $2,400/Wk
Weekly Spending
800
3,800
6,200
5,400
5,400
2,400
2,400
2,400
Cumulative Spending
800
4,600
10,800
16,200
21,600
24,000
26,400
28,800

it is derived directly from the schedule, it represents *planned performance* and therefore is called a *baseline plan.* Furthermore, since control is exercised by comparing progress to plan, this curve can be used as the basis for such comparisons so that the project manager can tell the status of the program. The next section presents examples of how such assessments are made.

Examples of Progress Tracking Using Spending Curves

Consider the curves shown in Figure 11-4. On a given date, the project is supposed to have involved $40,000 (40K) in labor (BCWS). The actual cost of the work performed (ACWP) is 60K. These figures are usually obtained from Accounting and are derived from all the time cards that have reported labor applied to the project. Finally, the budgeted cost of work performed (BCWP) is 40K. Under these conditions, the project would be behind schedule and overspent.

Figure 11-5 illustrates another scenario. The BCWP and the ACWP curves both fall at the same point, 60K. This means that the project is ahead of schedule but spending correctly for the amount of work done.

The next set of curves illustrates another status. In Figure 11-6, the BCWP and the ACWP curves are both at 40K. This means the project is behind schedule and under budget. However, because the manager spent 40K and got 40K of value for it, spend-

Figure 11-3. Cumulative spending for the sample bar chart.

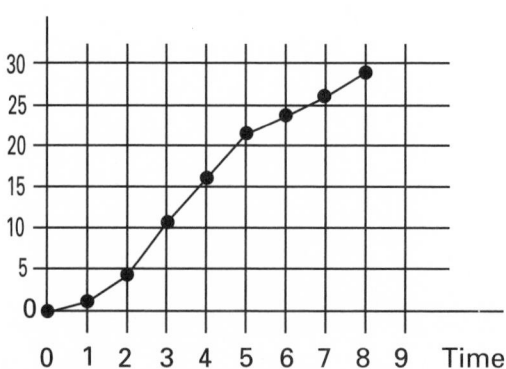

Figure 11-4. Plot showing project behind schedule and overspent.

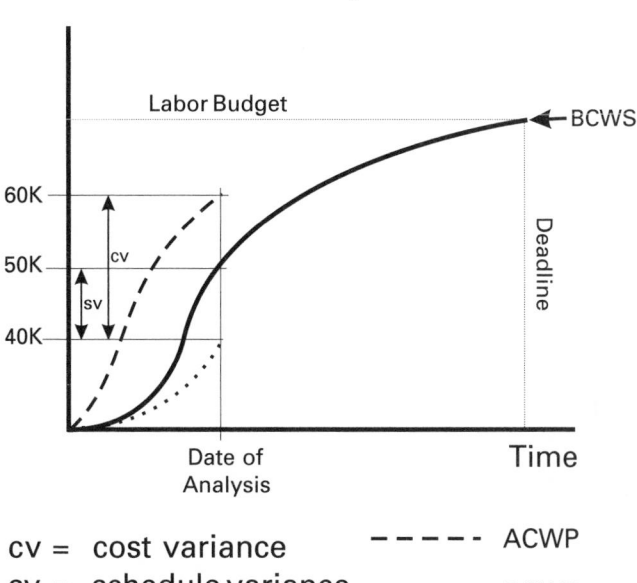

cv = cost variance   – – – – – ACWP
sv = schedule variance .... BCWP

Figure 11-5. Project ahead of schedule, spending correctly.

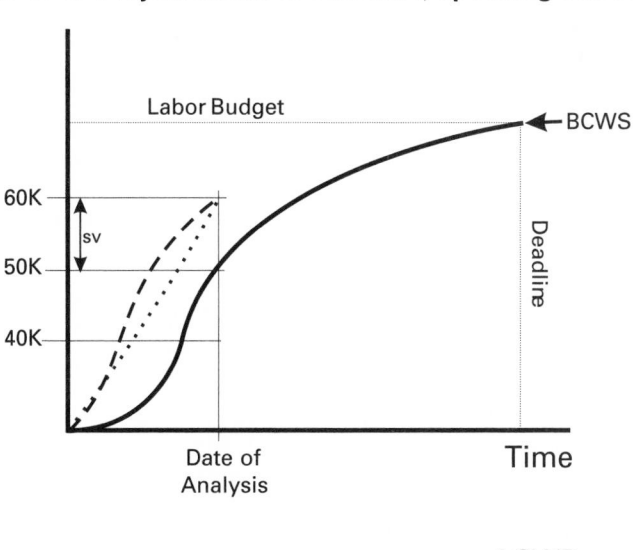

cv = cost variance   – – – – – ACWP
sv = schedule variance .... BCWP

ing is correct for what has been done. There is a *schedule variance*, but not a spending variance.

Figure 11-7 looks like Figure 11-4, except that the ACWP and the BCWP curves have been reversed. Now the project is ahead of schedule and underspent.

Variance Analysis Using Hours Only

In some organizations, project managers are held accountable not for costs but only for the hours actually worked on the project and for the work actually accomplished. In this case, the same analysis can be conducted by stripping the dollars off the figures. This results in the following:

▶ BCWS becomes Total Planned (or Scheduled) Hours

▶ BCWP becomes Earned Hours (Scheduled hours × % work accomplished)

▶ ACWP becomes Actual Hours Worked

Using hours only, the formulas become:

$$\text{Schedule Variance} = \text{BCWP} - \text{BCWS} =$$
$$\text{Earned Hours} - \text{Planned Hours}$$

$$\text{Labor Variance} = \text{BCWP} - \text{ACWP} =$$
$$\text{Earned Hours} - \text{Actual Hours Worked}$$

Tracking hours only does lead to one loss of sensitivity. ACWP is actually the composite of a labor rate variance times a labor-hours variance. When only labor-hours are tracked, you have no warning that labor rates might cause a project budget problem. Nevertheless, this method does simplify the analysis and presumably tracks the project manager only on what she can control.

Figure 11-6. Project is behind schedule but spending correctly.

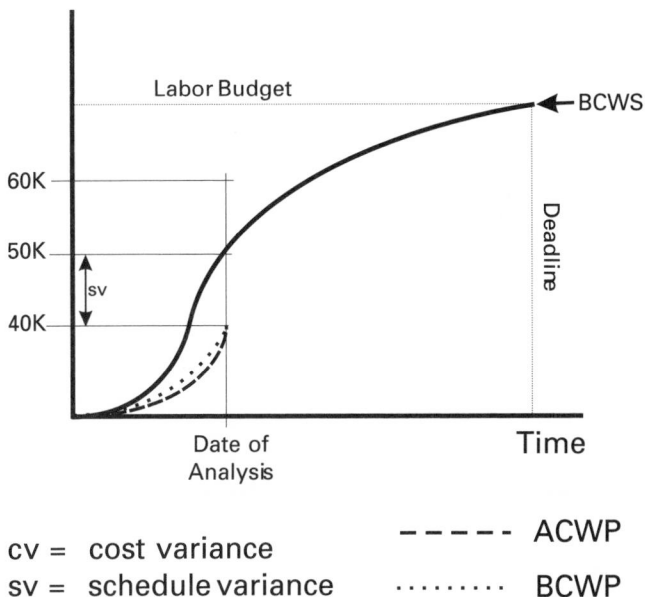

cv = cost variance   – – – – – ACWP
sv = schedule variance   ·········· BCWP

Figure 11-7. Project is ahead of schedule and underspent.

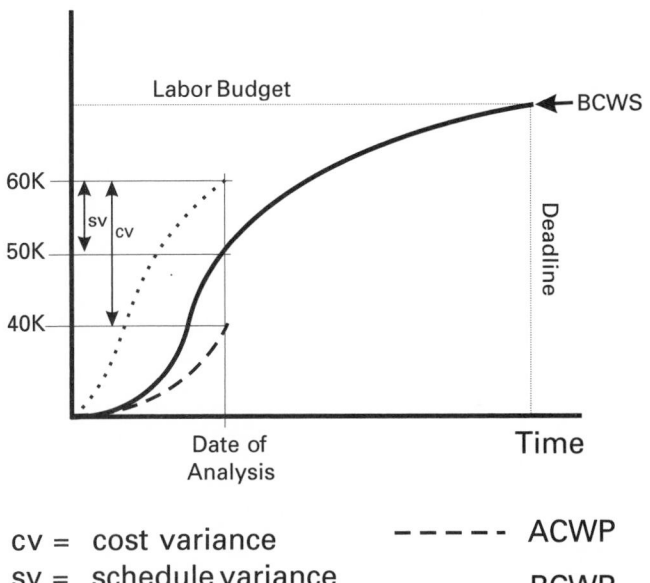

cv = cost variance   – – – – – ACWP
sv = schedule variance   ········· BCWP

Responding to Variances

It is not enough to simply detect a variance. The next step is to understand what it means and what caused it. Then you have to decide what to do to correct for the deviation. Earlier, I explained that there are four responses that can be taken when there is a deviation from plan. Which of these you choose depends in part on what caused the deviation. Following are some general guidelines:

▶ When ACWP and BCWP are almost equal and larger than BCWS (see Figure 11-5), it usually means that extra resources have been applied to the project, but at the labor rates originally anticipated. This can happen in several ways. Perhaps you planned for weather delays, but the weather has been good and you have gotten more work done during the analysis period than intended, but at the correct cost. Thus, you are ahead of schedule but spending correctly.

▶ When ACWP and BCWP are nearly equal and below BCWS (see Figure 11-6), it usually means the opposite of the previous situation; that is, you have not applied enough resources. Perhaps they were stolen from you, perhaps it has rained more than you expected, or perhaps everyone has decided to take a vacation at once. The problem with being in this position is that it usually results in an overspend when you try to catch up.

▶ When ACWP is below BCWS and BCWP is above BCWS (see Figure 11-7), you are ahead of schedule and underspent. This generally happens because the original estimate was too conservative (probably padded for safety). Another possibility is that you had a lucky break. You thought the work would be harder than it was, so you were able to get ahead. Sometimes it happens because people were much more efficient than expected. The problem with this variance is that it ties up resources that could be used on other projects. The economists call this an *opportunity cost*. There is also a good chance that if you were consistently padding estimates and were bidding against other companies on projects, you probably lost some bids. If your competitor is using average values for time estimates while you are padding yours, then your figures are likely to be higher, and you will lose the bid.

Acceptable Variances

What are acceptable variances? The only answer that can be given to this question is "It all depends." If you are doing a well-defined construction job, the variances can be in the range of ± 3–5 percent. If the job is research and development, acceptable variances increase generally to around ± 10–15 percent. When the job is pure research, the sky is the limit. Imagine, for example, that you worked for a pharmaceutical company and your boss said, "Tell me how long it will take and how much it will cost for you to discover and develop a cure for AIDS."

For every organization, you have to develop tolerances through experience. Then you start trying to reduce them. All progress is an attempt to reduce variation in what we do. We will never reduce it to zero unless we eliminate the process altogether, but zero has to be the target.

Using Percentage Complete to Measure Progress

The most common way to measure progress is to simply estimate percentage complete. This is the BCWP measure, but BCWP is expressed as a dollar value, whereas percentage complete does not make that conversion.

When percentage complete measures are plotted over time, you tend to get a curve like the one shown in Figure 11-8. It rises more or less linearly up to about 80 or 90 percent, then turns horizontal (meaning that no further progress is being made). It stays there for a while; then, all of a sudden, the work is completed.

Figure 11-8. Percent complete curve.

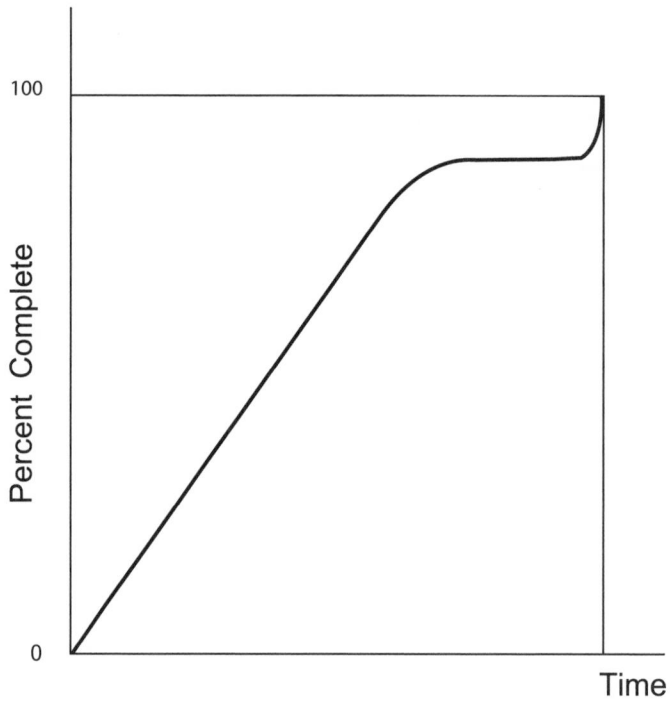

The reason is that problems are often encountered near the end of the task, and a lot of effort goes into trying to solve them. During that time, no progress is made.

Another part of the problem is in knowing where you are to begin with. We have already said that you are generally estimating progress. Consider a task that has a ten-week duration. If you ask the person doing that task where he is at the end of the first week, he is likely to tell you, "10 percent"; at the end of week two, "20 percent"; and so on. What he is doing is making a reverse inference. It goes like this: "It is the end of the first week on a ten-week task, so I must be 10 percent complete." The truth is, he really doesn't know where he is. Naturally, under such conditions, control is very loose. Still, this is the only way progress can be measured in many cases.

· ·
Key Points to Remember

▶ Control is exercised by analyzing from the plan.

▶ Well-defined projects can achieve tighter control over variations than poorly defined ones.

▶ There is a tendency to sacrifice quality when deadlines are difficult to meet.

▶ It is not enough to recognize a variance. Its cause must be determined so that corrective action can be taken.

▶ Acceptable variances can be determined only through experience. Every system has a capability. Your team may have the ability to maintain better tolerances on their work than another team.

· ·

Exercise ·

Consider the report in Figure 11-9, showing earned value figures for a project. Answer the questions by analyzing the data. Answers are provided in the Answers section at the back of the book.

Figure 11-9. Earned value report.

WBS #	Cumulative-to-date			Variance		At Completion		
	BCWS	BCWP	ACWP	SCHED.	COST	BUDGET	L. EST.	VARIANCE
301	800	640	880	−160	−240	2,400	2,816	−416

Questions:

1. Is the task ahead or behind schedule? By how much?

2. Is the task overspent or underspent? By how much?

3. When the task is completed, will it be overspent or underspent?

CHAPTER 12

Managing the Project Team

The previous chapters have concentrated primarily on the tools of project management—how to plan, schedule, and control the work. Unfortunately, far too many project managers see these tools as all they need to manage successfully. They assemble a team, give the members their instructions, then sit back and watch the project self-destruct. Then they question whether there might be some flaw in the tools.

In all likelihood, the problem was with how people were managed. Even in those cases where a problem with the tools may have existed, it is often the failure of people to properly apply them that causes the problem, so, again, we are back to people.

The tools and techniques of project management are a *necessary* but not a *sufficient* condition for project success. As I have stated, if you can't handle people, you will have difficulty managing projects, especially when the people don't "belong" to you.

Related to this is the need to turn a project *group* into a *team*. Far too little attention is paid to team building in project management. This chapter offers some suggestions on how to go about it.

Team Building

Building an effective team begins on the first day of the team's existence. Failure to begin the team-building process may result in a team that is more like a group than a team. In a group, members may be *involved* in but not *committed* to the activities of the majority.

Teams don't just happen—they must be built!

The problem of commitment is a major one for both organizations and project teams. It is especially significant in matrix organizations, in which members of the project team are actually members of functional groups and have their own bosses but report to the project manager on a "dotted-line" basis.

Later in this chapter, I present rules for how a project manager can develop commitment to a team. For now, let us turn to how to get a team organized so that it gets off to the right start. (For an in-depth treatment of this topic, see Jim Lewis's book *Team-Based Project Management.*)

Promoting Teamwork through Planning

A primary rule of planning is that those individuals who must implement the plan should participate in preparing it. Yet, leaders often plan projects by themselves, then wonder why their team members seem to have no commitment to the plans.

All planning requires some estimating—how long a task will take, given the availability of certain resources, and so on. In my seminars, I ask participants, "Do you often find that your boss thinks you can do your work much faster than you actually can?" They laugh and agree. As I tell them, it seems to be some kind of psychological law that bosses are optimistic about how long it will take their staffs to get a job done.

When a manager gives a person an assignment that allows inadequate time to perform, the individual naturally feels discouraged, and her commitment is likely to suffer. She might say, "I'll give it my best shot," but her heart isn't really in it.

Getting Organized

Here are the four major steps in organizing a project team:

1. Decide what must be done, using work breakdown structures, problem definitions, and other planning tools.

2. Determine staffing requirements to accomplish the tasks identified in the first step.

3. Recruit members for the project team.

4. Complete your project plan with the participation of team members.

Recruiting

Following are some of the criteria by which team members should be selected:

▶ The candidate possesses the skills necessary to perform the required work at the speed needed to meet deadlines.

▶ The candidate will have his needs met through participation in the project (see the March and Simon rules discussed later in this chapter).

▶ The applicant has the temperament to fit in with other team members who have already been recruited and with the project manager and other key players.

▶ The person will not object to overtime requirements, tight timetables, or other project work requirements.

Clarifying the Team's Mission, Goals, and Objectives

Peters and Waterman, in their book *In Search of Excellence*, have said that excellent organizations "stick to their knitting." They stick to what they are good at and do not go off on tangents, trying to do something they know nothing about. (Imagine, as an example, a hockey team deciding to play basketball.)

Numerous case studies and articles have been written about organizations that went off on tangents, at great cost, because they forgot their mission. The same can happen to project teams. If members are not clear on the team's mission, they will take the team where they think it is supposed to go, and that may not be the direction intended by the organization. The procedure for developing a mission statement is covered in Chapter 4, so no more will be said about it here. However, working with your team to develop a mission statement is a good team-building activity in itself.

> *If possible, the entire team should participate in developing the team's mission statement. This is a tremendous team-building activity in itself!*

Conflicts between Individual Goals and the Team's Mission

Experience has shown that team members are most committed to a team when their individual needs are being met. Sometimes members have what are called *hidden agendas*, personal objectives that they do not want anyone to know about, because they are afraid other members will try to block them if their objectives are known. Since a manager should try to help individual members achieve their personal goals, while achieving team goals as well, the team leader needs to bring hidden agendas into the open so that the individual can be helped to achieve his goal. Of course,

> *A manager should try to satisfy the needs of the organization, while simultaneously helping individuals satisfy their own needs through participation in the project.*

a person may occasionally have a goal that runs so counter to the team's goals that no reconciliation is possible. In that case, if the team leader can discover what the person's goal is, the individual can (ideally) be moved to another team in which his goal can be reached.

Team Issues

There are four general issues with which a team must deal. These are *goals*, *roles and responsibilities*, *procedures*, and *relationships*. In this chapter, we have dealt with clarifying the team's mission, goals, and objectives. This is *always* the first and most important step in developing a team.

Once that is done, people must understand their roles. These must be clearly defined. *What is expected* of each individual, and *by when*? The one problem that seems common is that team leaders think they clearly communicate this information to team members. Yet, when you ask team members if they are clear on their goals and roles, you frequently get a negative response.

The problem is with our failure to solicit feedback from team members in order to be sure that they understood; in addition, members themselves are sometimes reluctant to admit that they haven't understood. This appears to be a result of our tendency in school to put people down for asking "stupid questions." So, rather than admit that they don't understand, they *interpret* what they have been told and try to do the job the best they can.

Project leaders must establish a climate of open communication with the team in which no one feels intimidated about speaking up. The best way to do this is to comment on the problem: "I know some of you may feel reluctant to speak up and say you don't understand, but we can't operate that way. Please feel free to be candid. If you don't understand, say so. If you don't

> **Every team must deal with:**
>
> *goals*
>
> *roles and responsibilities*
>
> *procedures*
>
> *relationships*

agree with something, say so. That is the only way we can succeed. We will be lucky to have time to do the job once, much less find time to do it over because one of you failed to understand what was expected."

I have also found that people respond very positively when I am willing to admit that I don't understand something myself or am apprehensive or concerned about a project issue. If you project an air of infallibility, no one else is likely to admit a weakness. But, then, who wants to

> **There is no such thing as a stupid question—except perhaps the one you were afraid to ask.**

deal with a demigod? A little human frailty goes a long way toward breaking down barriers. I know this contradicts what some managers have been taught. The macho notion of infallibility has been with us for a long time, and I believe it is the cause of many of our organizational problems. It is time to abandon it for reality.

Working Out Procedures

Dealing with *how we do it* comes next. The key word here is *processes*. The work must be done as efficiently and as effectively as possible, and improvement of work processes is a very important issue today. It is commonly called *re-engineering* and is the analysis and improvement of work processes to make the organization more competitive.

The difficulty that most teams have with process is that they get so focused on doing the work that they forget to examine how it is done. Periodically, a team should stop working long enough to examine its processes and to see whether it could use better approaches. Otherwise, the team may get very good at doing the work badly.

> **So-called personality conflicts are often simply the result of people's lack of good interpersonal skills. This lack can be resolved through training.**

Relationships in Teams

Friction occurs in nearly every interaction between human beings. There are misunderstandings, conflicts, personality clashes, and petty jealousies. Project managers must be prepared to deal with these. In fact, if you really dislike having to deal with the behavioral problems that occur on projects, you should ask yourself whether you really want to manage projects at all. Like it or not, the behavioral problems come with the job, and failure to deal with them will sink a project eventually.

One thing to be aware of is that many personality clashes are the result of people's lack of good interpersonal skills. We have never been taught how to sit down and work out differences with others, so, when the inevitable conflict happens, the situation just blows up. The best way to minimize the impact of such problems is to provide training for all team members (including yourself) in interpersonal skills. This area has been sorely neglected in many organizations because there seems to be no bottom-line impact. It is hard to demonstrate that there will be a $10 return on a $1 training investment.

Because of our inability to quantify the benefits of skills training, we don't provide it. Yet, if we have capital resources that don't work well, we spend whatever is necessary to correct the problem. Interestingly, our *human resources* are the only ones that are renewable almost indefinitely, but we fail to take steps to keep them functioning effectively. As a project manager, you owe it to yourself to manage this aspect of the job.

Stages in a Team's Development

There are a number of models that describe the stages that teams or groups go through on the way to maturity. One of the more popular ones has self-explanatory titles for the stages: *forming, storming, norming,* and *performing.*

In the *forming* stage, people are concerned with how they will fit in and with who calls the shots, makes decisions, and so on. During this stage, they look to the leader (or someone else) to give them some *structure*—that is, to give them a sense of direction and to help them get started. A leader's failure to do this may result in loss of the team to some member who exercises what we call *informal leadership.*

The *storming* stage is frustrating for most people. When the team reaches this stage, people begin to question their goals. Are they on the right track? Is the leader really leading them? They sometimes play *shoot the leader* during this stage.

At the *norming* stage, they are beginning to resolve their conflicts and to settle down to work. They have developed *norms* (unwritten rules) about how they will work together, and they feel more comfortable with one another. Each individual has found her place in the team and knows what to expect of the others.

Finally, when the team reaches the *performing* stage, the leader's job is easier. Members generally work well together now, enjoy doing so, and tend to produce high-quality results. In other words, we can really call them a team at this point.

> **The most popular terms for the stages of team development are:**
>
> *forming*
>
> *storming*
>
> *norming*
>
> *performing*

Leading a Team through the Stages

A newly formed team needs considerable structure, or it will not be able to get started. As I noted in the previous section, a leader who fails to provide such structure during stage 1, the *forming* stage, may be rejected by the group, which will then look for leadership from someone else. A *directive* style of leadership is called for in the forming stage.

During this stage, members also want to get to know one another and want to understand the role each member will play on the team. In stage 1, the leader must help team members get to know one another and help them become clear

> **A *directive* style of leadership is called for when a team is in the forming stage.**

on goals, roles, and responsibilities. Leaders who are very task oriented tend to make a major error here: They just tell the team to "get to work," without helping members get to know one another. They view such purely "social" activities as a waste of time; surely members can attend to such things themselves. Although it seems obvious, it is hard to see yourself as a team when you don't know some of the "players."

Getting the team started with a kickoff party or dinner is one way to let members become acquainted in a purely social way, with no pressure to perform actual task work. If this is not feasible, there must be some mechanism for letting people get to know each other.

As the group continues to develop, it enters stage 2, *storming*. Here, people are beginning to have some anxiety. They start to question the group's goal: Are we doing what we're supposed to be doing? The leader must use *influence* or *persuasion* to assure them that they are indeed on track. They need a lot of psychological support, as well. They must be assured by the leader that they are valued, that they are vital to the success of the team, and so on. In other words, members need some stroking in this stage.

> **A selling or influence style of leadership is appropriate at the storming stage.**

There is a tendency to try to skip this stage, as managers feel uncomfortable with the conflict that occurs. To sweep such conflict under the rug and pretend that it doesn't exist is a mistake. The conflict must be *managed* so that it does not become destructive, but it must not be avoided. If it is, the group will keep coming back to this stage to try to resolve the conflict, and this will inhibit progress. Better to pay now and get it over with.

As the team enters stage 3, *norming*, it is becoming closer knit. Members are beginning to see themselves as a team

> **In the norming stage, the leader should adopt a participative style of leadership.**

and take some sense of personal identity from membership in the group. Members are now involved in the work, are becoming supportive of one another, and, because of their cooperation, can be said to be more of a team than a group at this point. The leader needs to adopt a *participative* style in this stage and share decision making more than in stages 1 and 2.

By the time a group reaches stage 4, *performing*, it is a real team. The leader can generally sit back and concentrate on what-if analysis of team progress, planning for future work, and so on. This is a *delegative* style of leadership and is appropriate. The team is achieving results, and members are usually taking pride in their accomplishments. In this stage, there should be signs of camaraderie, joking around, and real enjoyment in working together.

It is important to remember that no team stays in a single stage forever. If it encounters obstacles, it may drop back to stage 3, and the leader can no longer be delegative but must back up to the stage 3 management style, which is participative.

> **Delegative leadership is the proper style in the performing stage of a team's development. Note that delegative does not mean abdication!**

Membership in project teams often changes. When new members come on board, you should consider that for a short time the team will fall back to stage 1, and you will have to take it back through the stages until it reaches maturity again. It is *especially* important that you help everyone get to know the new member and understand what his role will be in the team. This does take some time, but it is essential if you want the team to progress properly.

Developing Commitment to a Team

At the beginning of this chapter, I pointed out that helping team members develop commitment to the project is a major problem for project managers. Team members are often assigned to a project simply because they are the best *available* people, not because they are the best people for the job. When this happens, they may have no commitment to the team.

In their book *Organizations*, March and Simon present five rules for developing commitment to a team or organization. Those rules are:

1. Have team members interact frequently so that they gain a sense of being a team.

2. Be sure that individual needs are being met through participation in the team.

3. Let all members know why the project is important. People don't like working on a "loser."

4. Make sure all members share the goals of the team. One bad apple can spoil the barrel.

5. Keep competition within the team to a minimum. Competition and cooperation are opposites. Let members compete with people outside the team, not within it.

Note that the first rule cannot always be followed if the team is scattered geographically. In that case, members should "meet" frequently through teleconferencing, videoconferencing, and/or an Internet-based tool. It is almost impossible to think of yourself as part of a team if the team never gets together in some manner.

Watch the movie Stand and Deliver for an excellent example of true leadership.

A Final Suggestion

If you want some good models of how to work with teams, take a look at the best coaches and see how they do it. Be careful, though, not to model the supermacho coach's behavior. That might work okay with a sports team, where people are there because they want to be there, but it is unlikely to work well with a project team where the members are there because they have to be. I also suggest that you watch the movie *Stand and Deliver* and see how Jaime Escalante deals with his kids. Then, the next time you are tempted to complain that you have a lot of responsibility and no authority, ask yourself how a teacher (who has even less authority than you do) can get a bunch of kids to work so hard. How did he get them to go to summer school or take math two periods a day? Then you will begin to realize what true leadership is all about.

Key Points to Remember

▶ Teams don't just happen—they must be built!

▶ Having the entire team participate in planning is one way to start the team-building process.

▶ Deal with *goals, roles and responsibilities, procedures,* and *relationships,* in that order.

▶ So-called personality conflicts are often caused by team members' poor interpersonal skills. For teams to function well, *all* members should receive training in this area.

▶ The style of leadership appropriate for a team depends on its stage of development. In the *forming* stage, it is directive. In *storming,* it is influencing. At the *norming* stage, switch to a participative style. Finally, when the team reaches the *performing* stage, you can be delegative.

CHAPTER 13

The Project Manager as Leader

Y ou must take an art and discipline approach in the project environment when leading your project team: the art of managing people and the discipline of applying the necessary project processes to be successful. I hear it all the time, because it is true. It has been my experience that the people factor can be and often is the most challenging part of the project equation. The project champion, team members, functional managers, subject matter experts, and virtually all stakeholders need to be effectively managed to ensure project success. Chapters 1 and 2 introduced definitions of generic leadership, and Chapter 12 related leadership style to the stages of project team development. Now I'm going to focus on what it means to be a project leader, understanding strengths and weaknesses, creating constituents, and understanding the

> There is a higher probability that things will accidentally go wrong in a project than that they will accidentally go right.

importance of motivation. I will also discuss conflict resolution, team synergies, and a practical approach to *leading* project meetings (not managing them).

Laying the Foundation

Before you can attempt to understand and lead others, you should invest in a meaningful self-inventory. I am not suggesting days of psychoanalysis but a practical look in the mirror at your own behavior and probable *drivers* of this behavior. This typically provides valuable insight regarding your actions, as well as those of your team members and other project stakeholders.

Understanding Leadership Characteristics

When leading project management seminars, I often ask the attendees to raise their hands if they have extra time on any given day. It is a rhetorical question, asked to emphasize the need to maximize every interaction. Given the frantic pace of the project environment, almost every encounter can be considered critical. An improved understanding of yourself and your stakeholders will lead to more efficient communication and better project leadership decisions. Your ability to persuade, motivate, and resolve conflicts will improve. When you *lay the foundation* regarding these people skills, you avoid behavioral misalignment with stakeholders on all levels. Your understanding of leadership characteristics—individual traits, strengths, and weaknesses—indicates how you should flex your style and adjust to the stakeholder and the situation. This produces better overall alignment, which leads to greater efficiency. In terms of best practice, the more *agile* you become, the greater the chance for project success.

> **An improved understanding of yourself and your stakeholders will lead to more efficient communication and better project leadership decisions.**

Understanding Leadership Styles

I have seen many projects fail because the project manager insists that stakeholders adjust to the leader's style. As mentioned earlier, project team maturation requires you to progress from the directive leadership style to the delegative approach. This is logical and applies to most team scenarios, emphasizing the need for flexibility in your approach. As you move through a typical project day, however, you are faced with many and varied interactions, requiring a smooth transition from one leadership style to the next. Some project leaders possess a natural aptitude for this, whereas others need to work at it. You should invest time and effort in developing this skill. Just as a chameleon changes skin color to maximize survival, so should you adjust your approach to people, situations, and circumstances to ensure project efficiency.

> Just as a chameleon changes skin color to maximize survival, so should you adjust your approach to people, situations, and circumstances to ensure project efficiency.

Most of us have a natural preferred style that we are comfortable with, aptly named the comfort zone. This can often make the transition from project manager to leader difficult to begin with. It is easy for you to operate when you are behaving naturally. When circumstances require you to break out of this area, though, it requires a certain amount of work. To be an effective project leader you should be cognizant of the reluctance you will probably encounter when changing your own behavior. If the directive style is indicated when dealing with a stakeholder and it happens to be your least preferred, make a conscience effort to be disciplined and nimble enough to modify your preferred approach and be direct. All of this attention to project leadership detail will result in improved alignment among your leadership style, your stakeholder's behavioral characteristics, and the numerous project scenarios encountered on a daily basis. Figure 13-1 presents a good visual context of this alignment:

Figure 13-1. Leadership style and alignment.

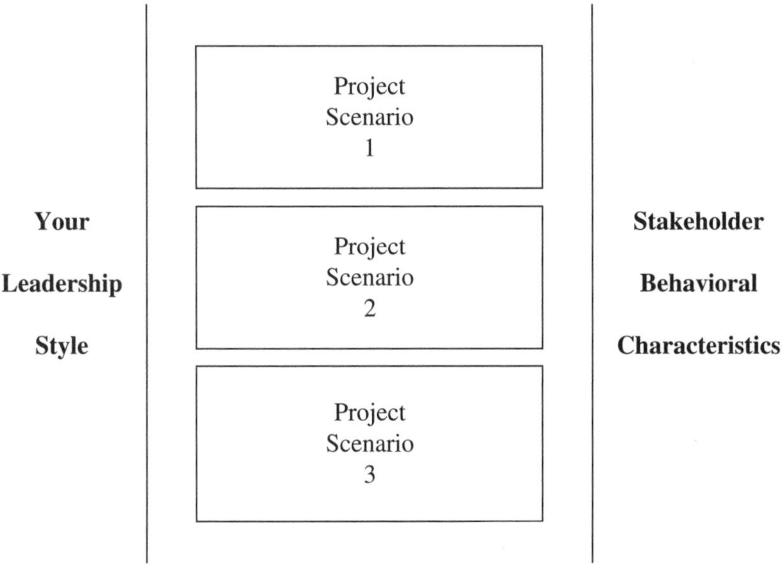

Creating Project Constituents

In the late twentieth century, very little attention was paid to the concept of project manager as leader. In a typical status meeting, team members reported progress regarding assigned action items (the same as today). If the work was not completed, the team member was often singled out, or perhaps his functional manager was called. Turnover was commonplace in the project team environment.

Times have changed. Effective project leadership is recognized by colleges, practitioners, and, yes, authors, as an integral part of overall project success. The rise of project-based organizations (in which most work is accomplished through projects), the virtual nature and reach of global projects, and cultural diversity have all contributed to the demand for better leaders, not just managers of teams. Leaders need constituents, and project leaders are no exception.

Creating a Consistency in Working Relationships

To create a *constituency*, team members and stakeholders who enthusiastically perform or support the project work, you need to engender trust and respect, perhaps even admiration. It is important to "walk the talk" and establish a consistency in working relationships. For example, if a coach in any sport employs a fiery, demanding style and then abandons it midseason, the team will be confused and confounded, and its performance will likely suffer. Constituents do not expect perfection, but most require consistency from their project leaders. If you adopt this approach, it will have a positive effect on team and stakeholder morale.

> It is important to "walk the talk" and establish a consistency in working relationships.

Encouraging Risk Taking and the Elimination of Fear of Failure

As project leader, you should encourage risk taking and try to eliminate the fear of failure. If the team is afraid to make mistakes, its ability to perform at a high level will be impeded. It is important to leverage everyone's knowledge and capability to maximize members' contribution to the project. Although it sounds counterintuitive, mistakes can present important opportunities. Not only can you learn from your mistakes, but you can use them to mold behavior and set the tone of the team environment. During my career as project leader, one of the best practices that I learned was to take advantage

> Although it sounds counterintuitive, mistakes can present important opportunities. Not only can you learn from your mistakes, but you can use them to mold behavior and set the tone of the team environment.

of the first mistake I made. I would announce what I did wrong, say, "My bad," and then explain how I intended to fix the problem. If team members see that you are open and willing to share your missteps, chances are excellent that they will act accordingly and be willing to take prudent risks as the project proceeds.

Establishing a Positive Culture of Dissent

"All titles are left at the door" is one of the first statements I make when meeting with the team for the first time. This is an important ground rule that will help you establish a *positive culture of dissent*. If the project is in the second phase, *storming*, and meetings are overly cordial and agreeable, you have a problem. This is, in all likelihood, a dysfunctional team that is operating in a constricted environment. This does not mean that you encourage conflict, but you will want to promote a variety of perspectives. As project leader, it is important for you to create an environment that encourages the exchange of ideas and opinions, free of the threat of reprisals. This positive culture of dissent helps you keep ideas flowing and assists you in making strategic and tactical decisions. If you are surrounded by "yes" people, devoid of the necessary vetting of ideas, the project will most likely stagnate, and you will lose the real value of your constituents.

Motivation

All project managers require team members to complete activities and accomplish work on time. As an effective project leader, you need to add an additional element—maximum performance. Getting the most from your team requires you to focus on team members as individuals, not just a collective of workers meeting deadlines. If you motivate the individuals, you motivate the team and establish the foundation for a high-performance environment. Conversely, an unmotivated project team will have difficulty succeeding regardless of how the technical aspects of the project are managed.

Some project leads use self-assessment tools to identify traits and possible motivational triggers of the team members. While these have proven to be effective in many instances, I prefer the more traditional approach of spending time with team members and other key stakeholders to find out what makes them tick. If you invest time to speak and listen to team members over coffee on a Tuesday morning (try to avoid Mondays, as some of us need to adjust from the weekend) and acknowledge the contributions of colleagues over a beverage at happy hour or an occasional lunch, you will strengthen the relationship and usually gain insight into who they are. The more you know, the better equipped you will be when the need to motivate arises. MBWA, or management by walking around, was introduced in the 1970s by Bill Hewlett and Dave Packard and became known as "the Hewlett-Packard (HP) style." It stresses this technique and is still practiced by project leaders, CEOs, and managers at all levels because it works. This is especially true in the typical project environment where the leader is managing without formal authority. If you lack the authority to tell them, you need the ability to motivate them.

Celebrate. As soon as possible, an accomplishment, big or small, should be acknowledged and celebrated as a team. As projects begin, a certain amount of inertia must be overcome. Start by celebrating the small victories, and, as the project progresses, continue to acknowledge good work as appropriate. Many project leaders celebrate with the team as milestones are reached or predetermined goals are accomplished at the end of each project phase. Whichever method you employ, it is your job to keep the momentum going by knowing your team and ensuring high morale.

> **It is your job to keep the momentum going by knowing your team and ensuring high morale.**

Project Leadership and the Team Environment

As mentioned earlier, the idea of the project manager as leader is a relatively new concept. In the recent past, team member roles, conflict-resolution strategies, and synergies were not considered critical to overall project success. As a project leader today, you need to address all of these areas. This section highlights proven techniques for leading project teams and expands the focus to include distributed virtual teams.

Identifying and Developing Team Member Roles

Although you represent the glue that holds the team together, you can also be thought of as the chef who is responsible for mixing the ingredients of project team member roles, skill sets, and personalities to maximize overall performance. Yes, it's a mixed metaphor, but it illustrates an important concept. As the project progresses, individuals often assume roles that fit naturally into the team environment with little or no resulting conflict. In other cases, it becomes evident that the chemistry is not right, resulting in daily clashes and negative dissent. In today's project world, you need to identify team member strengths, weaknesses, traits, and patterns to establish lasting project rapport. Each team member is present for a purpose, usually functional or subject matter expertise.

In order for the team to gel, you must observe the dynamics of the group. Be proactive and identify danger zones where potential conflicts may occur. Look for opportunities to coordinate team member efforts or even form subteams to leverage their combined talents. Your goal is to promote synergies for maximum team performance. A common definition of *synergy* reads: "The whole is greater than the sum of its parts." As project team leader, this is something for you to strive for, and it is a full-time job.

Determining the Appropriate Approach to Conflict Resolution

All project teams experience conflict at some point, and, as I emphasized earlier, much of it is healthy and positive. It is when conflict becomes destructive to project work and relationships that you need to take action. Personality issues, conflicting priorities, stakeholder disagreement, tight schedules, and technical issues all can be considered root causes of conflict in the project environment. How you deal with the issues that arise will be a determining factor in your effectiveness as project leader. Most of us develop our own style for dealing with conflict. As mentioned earlier in the chapter, this can lead to a comfort zone that hinders your ability to flex your style to fit the situation. Susan Junda presented five approaches to address conflict in the project environment (*Project Team Leadership: Building Commitment Through Superior Communication*; American Management Association, 2004).

1. *Avoidance.* Often called the *flight* syndrome, avoidance occurs when an individual delays the issue, withdraws from the situation, or avoids the conflict altogether.

2. *Accommodating.* In this instance, an individual focuses on meeting the needs of the other person, to the exclusion of everything else.

3. *Compromising.* This is an attempt to find the *middle ground* in which neither party gets all that it is seeking.

4. *Collaborating.* Here, both parties work together to come to a mutually beneficial solution; this is typically a *win-win* scenario.

5. *Forcing/Competing.* This is the "my way or the highway" approach, when one individual forges ahead with his idea.

Your task is to determine which approach is most appropriate given the project conflict scenario. If you have invested yourself in truly understanding your project constituents, this task becomes less difficult. External conflicts require that you make a more thorough assessment of the situation and individual(s) before you make an informed decision. Whichever approach you choose, remember to focus on the facts, not the emotions.

Leading Project Status Meetings

The importance of project status meetings is underrated. Yes, most organizations hold too many meetings that take up too much time, but status meetings are critical to your project's success. If every CEO realized the amount of time and money wasted on inefficient meetings, everybody would be trained to be effective meeting leaders and participants. You as project leader are responsible for making your status meetings efficient, effective, and productive.

Here are some best practices for efficiently run project status meetings:

> *Status* the work; don't expend valuable time *accomplishing* the work in the meeting.

> Establish meeting ground rules such as:

- Minimum number of members for a quorum (enough to hold the meeting).
- Consensus (in case of a deadlock, if five members agree, then the meeting proceeds, with the possibility to revisit the issue).
- All titles are left at the door (this is worth mentioning again).
- Confidentiality (everything said stays in the meeting room).
- One person speaks at a time.

> Start on time; end on time.

> Appoint a timekeeper to help you keep to your schedule.

> Recruit a scribe to record and distribute meeting minutes.

> Focus on participation to ensure that every voice is heard.

> Do not allow extended sidebar discussions.

> Ensure that all electronic devices are off or on vibrate.

> **You as project leader are responsible for making your status meetings efficient, effective, and productive.**

When establishing ground rules, it is important to include *all* team members to ensure buy-in. If you try to dictate these to the team, nobody will adhere to them. Some project teams alternate the role of scribe. This is a bad idea. If you appoint a single scribe, that individual will develop efficient habits of recording and distributing the minutes in a timely manner. If the job rotates to share the work, each week will produce a different style, and no single team member will develop the aforementioned efficiencies.

Working with Virtual Teams

"Brussels, we have a problem." I remember saying these words to a team member following my previous decision to suspend weekly videoconferencing. I did not understand the communication challenges that were facing my global team at the time. Needless to say, the decision was reversed. If your team resides in other buildings or is spread across the globe, you should identify your specific challenges and plan to overcome them.

Most virtual teams encounter blockages that are unique or that are much more likely in a geographically dispersed environment. Communication on every level can become an art, a science, a circus, or a torment. When team members are not down the hall or upstairs, clarification can become a project in itself. Things tend to get lost in translation. They fall through the ever-present but often unseen cracks. Add multicultural or multilingual team members, and factions can develop along those lines. Cultural differences, if not identified but left to fester, can prevent the development of real team unity. Differences in work habits, protocol, and style are more common and consequential.

Communication on every level can become an art, a science, a circus, or a torment.

To combat these added challenges, you must go back to basics when it comes to understanding your team members and stakeholders. Insist that the project kickoff meeting be face-to-face. This may prove *very* difficult, especially when extensive travel is involved, but it is crucial to team bonding and future morale. You will find that this is something that must be *sold* to management or the project champion. If this is the case, estimate projected costs and benefits and present them as often as necessary (it once took me six attempts until I got a "yes").

If your organization is lacking the latest virtual communication tools, become a squeaky wheel. Sell the need to invest in upgrades by highlighting the costs and negative effects of outdated programs on previous projects.

As the project progresses, it can also be useful to facilitate as many opportunities for informal interaction among team members as possible. This helps overcome the loss of casual interaction and assists in breaking down barriers.

Key Points to Remember

▶ The more agile you become in leading others, the greater the chance for project success.

▶ It is important to "walk the talk" and establish consistency in your working relationships. Encouraging risk taking, eliminating fear of failure, and establishing a positive culture of dissent will make you a more effective project leader.

▶ It is your job to keep the momentum going by knowing your team and ensuring high morale.

▶ As a project leader, you need to be able to identify and develop team member roles, determine the appropriate approach to conflict resolution, lead project status meetings, and work with virtual teams.

Exercise

Analyze the project environment in your organization. Make a list of ten important project leadership characteristics that help ensure success. From that list, identify the three most important characteristics. Then contrast the list with your own abilities. Which characteristics are your strongest? Which areas may need improvement?

CHAPTER 14

How to Make Project Management Work in Your Company

I

t is one thing to know how to manage projects. It is another to get people to actually *do* the work of the project. Running by the seat of the pants seems a lot easier than doing all the planning, scheduling, and monitoring that have been presented in this book. Even when people invest three or four days in project management seminars, you find that they soon forget what they have been taught and go back to the old ways.

I have struggled with this problem for twenty years and finally have some answers. Here are suggestions on how to make the principles of project management work in your company:

▶ Dr. W. Edwards Deming learned more than fifty years ago that if you don't get top management involved in a program, the program will be short lived. This doesn't mean just having them pay lip service to it. As Tom Peters suggests in his book *Thriving on Chaos*, if an executive wants something to happen in the company, she has to change her calendar; she must spend time talking about project management, sit in on project planning or review meetings, start asking to see people's project notebooks, and ask questions about how projects are doing. In other words, she must show an interest in the subject.

▶ Companies must build into performance appraisals items that evaluate a project manager's use of the best management tools. They should reward people for practicing the best methods and, if necessary, sanction them when they do not. But be careful. Be sure upper management is not keeping managers from practicing good methodology.

▶ It helps to have the entire team trained in the basics. After all, when you tell members of your team that you want them to do a WBS for their part of the project and they've never even heard the term before, they can't very well deliver. I have found that project managers generally need a minimum of three or four days' training in project management, and team members need about two days' training.

▶ I have found that senior management should have a brief overview of the principles so that it knows what it is realistic to expect. One of the most common causes of project failures is unrealistic expectations on the part of senior managers. However, I have found that most senior managers are so busy that you can get them together for only about three hours—if you can even do that. We have finally videotaped a briefing and cut it down to one hour and fifteen minutes, just enough time for busy executives to learn what they need to know to support and drive the effort. Today, senior managers should take advantage of the many online training options available to them.

▶ After the training is complete, pick a project that already has a pretty high probability of success—don't pick your hardest job; the probability of failure is too high—and have your trainer/consultant walk the team through the steps. This is the handholding phase, and I have found it to be essential (as have a number of major companies with which I have worked). It really helps to have someone assist the team in practicing what it has learned. All new procedures feel awkward when you first try them, and an outside expert makes things go smoother. In addition, an outsider can be more objective than members of the team.

▶ Plan small wins for people. Forget the Pareto principle. It's wrong in this particular instance, even from an economic point of view. According to Pareto, you should begin with your most important problems and solve them, then move on to the simpler ones. Sounds like good economic sense, but it isn't. It ignores the fact that the biggest problem is also likely to be the hardest to tackle, so people are more likely to fail, become demoralized, and give up. No sports team ranked tenth would want to play the top-ranked team for its first game. It would prefer to play the ninth-ranked team maybe, or even the eleventh. Don't set the team up to be slaughtered!

▶ Practice a lot of MBWA (management by walking around) as the project progresses, but do it to be helpful, not in the blame-and-punishment mode. Give people strokes for letting you know about problems early, not after they have turned into disasters. Don't be too quick to help people, though. Give them time to solve the problems themselves. Just ask them to keep you informed, and tell them to let you know if they need help. Be a resource, not a policeman.

▶ Do process reviews to learn and to try to improve whenever possible.

▶ If you find you have a problem child on your team, deal with that person as soon as possible. If you don't know how to handle the problem, talk to someone who has the experience and who can help you. Don't ignore the problem, as it can wreck your entire team.

▶ Be very *proactive*, not reactive. Take the lead. Break roadblocks for your team members. Go to bat for them.

▶ Have team members make presentations to senior management on their part of the job. Give them credit for their contributions. Build ownership.

▶ If you are running a project where people are assigned temporarily but still report to their own bosses (the matrix organization), keep their managers informed about what they are doing. Try to build good relations with those managers. You may need their support to get the job done.

▶ For those tasks on the critical path of the project, you may find that you have to strategically locate the people doing those activities so that you don't have them constantly pulled off to do other jobs. Major corporations are using this method more and more today on highly important projects.

▶ It may be useful to consider setting up a *project support person* or *office* to do all scheduling for your project managers. Rather than have everyone try to master the software, it may be better to train one or two people to competence level, with users trained only enough to know the capability of the software. Under this scenario, project managers give raw data to the support group, which enters them into the computer and then gives back the schedule; the schedule is then massaged until it works. Subsequently, the support group does all updates, what-if analyses, and so on for the project manager.

▶ Along this line, have a person assigned as *project administrator*. This person either does the project support or delegates it. He also sits in on project review meetings, holds the team's hands to walk members through planning and audits, and so forth. Naturally, you need to be running quite a few projects (at least ten to twenty) to justify this position. Such a person can be helpful when the people who are managing projects have little experience with managing or perhaps have poor skills for dealing with people, or both.

▶ Benchmark other companies to find out what they do with project management. Note that, when you find companies that don't practice good methodology, this does not give you grounds for abandoning good practices yourself. I know of one major corporation that does not track actual work put into a project; yet the company is extremely successful. However, the fact that it doesn't track work is going to lead to problems eventually. The company does a lot of other things really well, however, and I would not hesitate to benchmark those things.

▶ Have individuals take responsibility for being *champions* of various parts of the project management process. Perhaps you can make one person the earned value champion, who goes around the company trying to get everyone on board so that all team members all use the same method. Another could take responsibility for dealing with WBS notation, and so on.

▶ Join the Project Management Institute, attend its chapter meetings, and learn more about project management from other professionals.

▶ Try to read current management books, and glean everything you can from them that will help you do your job better. Managing projects is a demanding job, and you need all the help you can get.

▶ Consider changing the structure of the organization to one that is project based. Tell all functional managers that they exist to serve the needs of projects. Many of them will scream. Some may even quit. But, in today's world, where most of what gets done in organizations is in project format, this makes good sense.

▶ Set up a project management function, with dedicated project managers. You don't have everyone doing accounting. Not everyone is good at it. This is also true of project management. By making it a function, like all the others, you provide a way for dedicated individuals to hone their skills and get really good at the job. An excellent resource for this is Robert Graham and Randall L. Englund, *Creating an Environment for Successful Projects.*

▶ Look at managing projects as a *challenge* or even as a game. If it doesn't strike you that way, it probably won't be very exciting. Experiment with new approaches. Find out what works, and keep it. Throw out what does not.

Finally—good luck!

Answers to Chapter Questions

Chapter 1

1. c
2. d
3. a
4. b

Chapter 3

You should decide on project strategy before you begin implementation planning. At that point, you should develop tactics to execute strategy and plan logistics so that people will have what they need to execute the tactics.

Chapter 6

WBS for camping trip:

Figure A-1. WBS for camping trip.

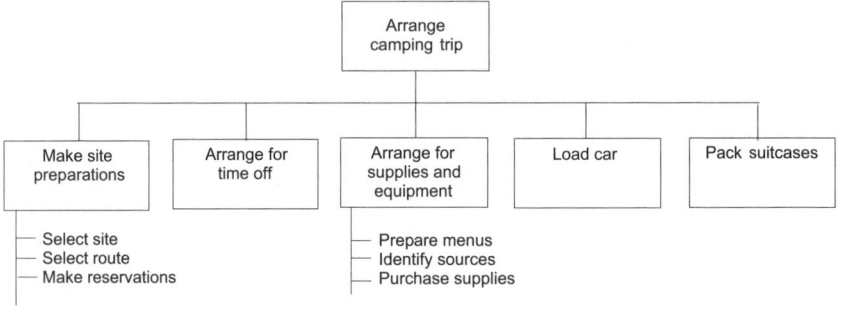

Chapter 7

Solution to the WBS exercise:

Figure A-2. Solution to the WBS exercise.

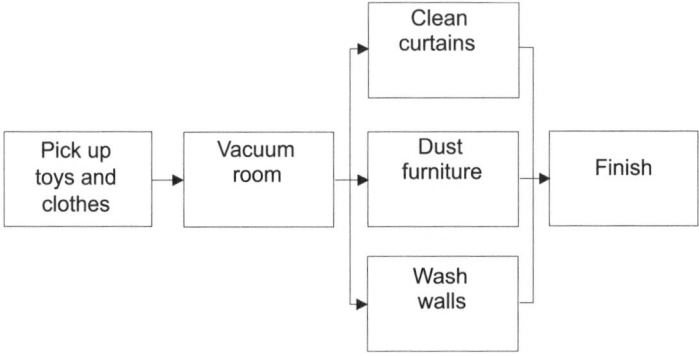

Chapter 8

Solution to the scheduling exercise:

Figure A-3. Solution to the scheduling exercise.

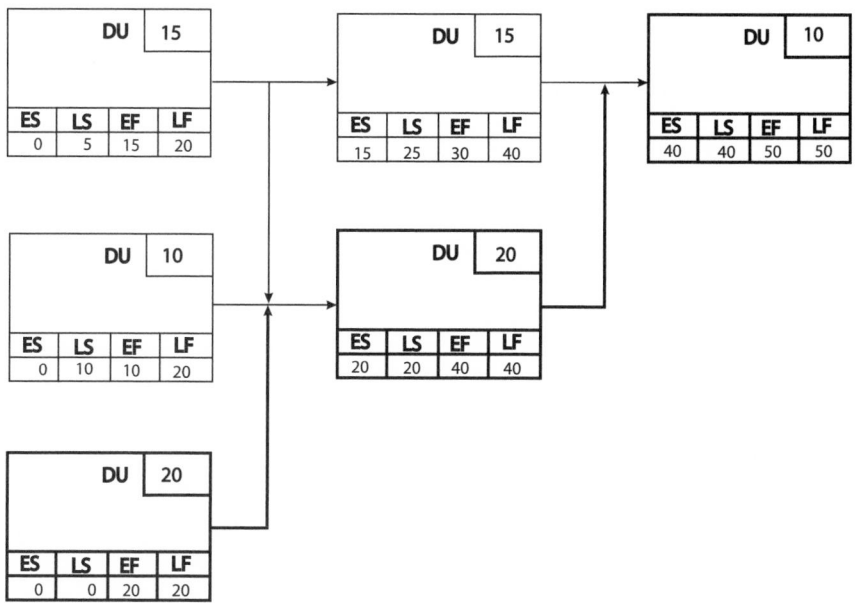

Chapter 11

1. It is behind schedule by $160 worth of work.

2. It is overspent by $240.

3. It will be overspent by $416.

INDEX

About the Authors

Joseph Heagney has been President of QMA International, LLC, since 2001, providing a wide range of management learning solutions worldwide. He specializes in delivering seminars to *Fortune* 500 companies and speaking at selected conferences and conventions. His clients have included PepsiCo, Federal Express, Verizon, Merck, Harvard Business School, the U.S. Armed Forces, and SAP Americas.

Mr. Heagney joined the American Management Association International (AMA) in 1996 as a Program Manager overseeing manufacturing, quality, and purchasing public seminar product lines. Following a transition to the project management product line, he was named Group Program Manager for the Center for Management Development in New York City and managed program managers in the areas of project management, training and development, communication, purchasing, and general management. Promoted to Global Practice Leader, Project Management Best Practices, he led an international team responsible for identifying and then incorporating best practices into AMA learning solutions content worldwide.

He is also an adjunct instructor at the City University of New York and the Dowling Institute/Dowling College, New York, on both the graduate and the undergraduate levels. He currently teaches multiple on-site courses in Dowling's Executive MBA Program. Courses taught include Project Management, Production and Operations Management, Operations Research, Leadership, General Management, Human Management Systems, Total Quality Management, Statistical Quality/ Statistical Process Control, and Executive Development.

He began his career with Grumman Aerospace (Northrop Grumman), where he advanced through the Material Management and Corporate Procurement Divisions. He completed his career at Northrop Grumman leading a project team to create and implement a corporatewide supplier performance rating system.

Mr. Heagney holds a Bachelor of Science degree in Education from C.W. Post College and a Master of Science degree in Industrial Management from SUNY Stony Brook. His professional affiliations have included the Project Management Institute, the International Project Management Association, and the American Society for Quality.

Fundamentals of Project Management would not be the best-selling title it has been without **James P. Lewis, PhD,** the author of the first three editions. Dr. Lewis is president of The Lewis Institute, Inc., a training and consulting company specializing in project management, which he founded in 1981. An experienced project manager, he teaches seminars on the subject throughout the United States, England, and the Far East.

Since 1980, Dr. Lewis has trained more than thirty thousand supervisors and managers in Argentina, Canada, England, Germany, India, Indonesia, Malaysia, Mexico, Singapore, Sweden, Thailand, and the United States. He has written articles for *Training and Development Journal, Apparel Industry Magazine,* and *Transportation and Distribution Magazine.* He is the author of *Project Planning, Scheduling and Control, Mastering Project Management, The Project Manager's Desk Reference,* and *Working Together: The 12 Principles Employed by Boeing Commercial Aircraft to Manage Projects, Teams, and the Organization,* published by McGraw-Hill, and, in addition to this book, *How to Build and Manage a Winning Project Team* and *Team-Based Project Management,* published by AMACOM Books. He is also coauthor, with Bob Wysocki, of *The World-Class Project Manager,* published by Perseus.

Announcing!

AMACOM's Best-Selling Project Management Titles

101 Project Management Problems and How to Solve Them	*$19.95*
Emotional Intelligence for Project Managers	*$19.95*
Fundamentals of Project Management, Fourth Edition	*$16.95*
Identifying and Managing Project Risk	*$32.95*
Improving Your Project Management Skills	*$15.00*
Rescue the Problem Project	*$32.95*
Results without Authority	*$19.95*
Succeeding in the Project Management Jungle	*$19.95*
The AMA Handbook of Project Management	*$79.95*
The Little Black Book of Project Management, Third Edition	*$16.00*
The Project Management Took Kit, Second Edition	*$19.95*

Visit www.amacombooks.org
for these and other useful books for your life on the job!

Prices subject to change.

Announcing!